Dedication

I dedicate this book to all the personal trainers in our industry who are making a difference in so many people's lives.

Acknowledgments

As with any piece of work, numerous people have provided support, feedback and guidance. They all deserve recognition.

I would like to express my extreme gratitude to the team at IDEA. I appreciate their ongoing support. Peter, Kathie, Pat, Aprile, Kristen, April and all the others I've worked with over the years are all exceptional examples of what professionalism is all about. My thanks go out to my teachers, colleagues and role models who have, collectively, provided me with the knowledge, tools and experiences to present this material: Maureen Hagan, David Patchell-Evans, Matt Church, Gregory Florez, Bob Esquerre, Ken Baldwin, Susan Cantwell, Michael Youssouf, Scott McLain, Jeff Munger, and the team at The Fitness Group. I would also like to thank IDEA, IHRSA, Can-Fit-Pro and other fitness associations for their commitment to providing fitness leaders with the education we need to do our jobs effectively and safely.

I'd like to thank the *Province Newspaper*, *Chatelaine Magazine*, RainCoast Publishers, and other trade journals and publications for allowing me the opportunity to develop my writing skills so I could competently finish this book.

I'd also like to thank Nike and PowerBar for their continuous support and belief in my vision.

And, of course, we all appreciate the additional contributions made by the businesses that provided the samples and marketing tips in this book: Donna Hutchinson, On The Edge Fitness Consulting; Michele Colwell, GoodLife Fitness Clubs; Justin Tamsett, Active Fitness; Julie McNeney, The Fitness Group; Nikki and Andrew Ellis, City Personal Training; Maureen Wilson, Sweat Co Workout Studios; Neil Chasan, Sports Reaction Center; Colin Westerman, Fitness by Colin Westerman; and Ingrid Knight-Cohee, FIT-JETS.

My husband, Alex, friends and family have supported me unconditionally in all my pursuits—I love all of them so much.

And last, but definitely first, I'd like to give all the thanks to God for His many blessings and for my ability to work in a field I am so passionate about.

"We opened a brand new, state-of-the-art medical fitness center in June of 1996. Sherri was recruited to train our staff on how to upsell their personal training services. When she started, the program was averaging only $10,000 per month in revenue. Today, our program has grown to over $70,000 per month! Sherri made a huge impact on our team of employees."

Darrell McKay, Director of Integrated Wellness Services
Ellerbe Becket, USA

"Sherri's marketing, advertising, sales and customer service systems have been invaluable to our personal training department. Our business was losing money and she helped turn it around so that last year we experienced an annual turnover of $168K and a profit of $25K. This year, we're already enjoying a quarterly turnover of $50K and a profit of around 18%."

Justin Tamsett, Owner, Active Fitness Group
Sydney, Australia

"Since implementing many of Sherri's business ideas, our personal training revenue has increased by over 120%."

David Wu, Managing Partner
The London Athletic Clubs, London, Ontario

"Sherri increased personal training revenues for our business tenfold, created numerous group personal training programs and activities and implemented invaluable systems that helped us get and keep clients. She helped to bring our personal training program to world-class level."

Julie McNeney, VP Marketing, The Fitness Group
1999 IDEA Program Director of the Year

"Sherri's book will provide the reader with her personal insight and research into marketing and structuring a successful personal training business. This is a must for the beginning-to-grow company looking to leap ahead of the competition by increasing the bottom line and providing great customer service."

Ken Baldwin, MEd, President, Premier Fitness Inc.
1999 IDEA/Life Fitness Personal Trainer of the Year

"Certainly a shining star in the fitness industry, Sherri McMillan shares her marketing tactics in an easy-to-follow, comprehensive step-by-step workbook. This book is a 'must read' for any trainer who wants to thrive rather than simply survive!"

Michael Youssouf
2000 IDEA Personal Trainer of the Year

The Successful
Trainer's Guide to
Marketing

How to get clients
and SAVE money!

by Sherri McMillan, MSc

IDEA Personal Trainer of the Year, 1998

IDEA
HEALTH & FITNESS ASSOCIATION

Library of Congress Catalog Card Number 13-6580

ISBN-10: 1-887781-04-8

ISBN-13: 978-1-887781-04-6

Editor:	Patricia Ryan
Copy Editor:	Colleen Sharp
Designer:	Lorie Kennedy
Cover Photography:	The Stock Market

Printed in the United States of America

IDEA Press
10455 Pacific Center Court
San Diego, CA 92121-4339
phone: (858) 535-8979, (800) 999-4332
fax: (858) 535-8234
www.ideafit.com

Introduction

If you love what you do, you never have to *work* another day in your life!

My career is based on the above statement. Wouldn't you hate to wake up every morning dreading going to work? Luckily, in our industry, most of us love what we do.
In fact, based on an IDEA survey, 88% of personal trainers are satisfied with their career choices. It makes you feel good to know you're making such a huge difference in so many people's lives, doesn't it? But here's the depressing part: Only 49% of us are satisfied with how much money we make. Yet you don't have to settle for a low income. You can love what you do *and* be compensated well.

I am often astonished at what other professionals charge for their services. For example, my lawyer charges $250 per hour. And nothing against lawyers, but what does he do for me besides shuffle some papers and file a bunch of forms? Professionals such as lawyers can charge their enormous fees because they act like professionals. They conduct their businesses using very professional systems. And, of course, these professionals' clients need them.

But don't our clients need us too? And isn't someone's health and fitness just as important as—if not more important than—monotonous legal affairs? If we expect to be compensated like professionals, we have to position our business professionally. This includes paying particular attention to our marketing and advertising systems, sales skills, customer service systems, educational background and personality development. Once we position personal training as a credible and reputable business, we can be justified in charging higher fees and making a larger income.

When I first started personal training in the '80s, it was easy to succeed. There was very little competition so I could easily position myself as an expert. Setting up professional systems made it easy for me to attract clients, sell them and then keep them. Today, the IDEA/ASD survey estimates there are 55,000 personal trainers practicing in the United States alone, and there are many in Canada. The competition is fierce and is growing rapidly. In fact, 92% of fitness clubs now offer some form of personal training; many trainers operate businesses independent of clubs; and personal training studios are opening in communities all over
North America. The competition makes it even more important for personal trainers to stay on the cutting edge of the industry and look for ways to take their business to the next level.

When writing this book, I made an assumption: Your personal training career is just beginning and you need clients; you have a few clients but want more; or you are a veteran trainer with a full client base who wants to keep the clients you've got. If you fall into any of these categories, you will learn things that will help you succeed in the personal training industry.

To me, "wealthy" personal trainers are not just wealthy financially, they also enjoy a different kind of wealth as a result of the impact they make on people's lives. After reading and applying many of the principles I am going to present in this book, your business will be wealthy in all definitions of the word.

Good luck, and I will pray for your continued success and happiness!

Sherri
xo

Table of Contents

CHAPTER ONE
Who Are You?

Failing to plan is planning to fail.

Have you heard the story of the Canadian lumberjack? He was a very strong man who took pride in his work. One day he went into the forest to chop trees. His muscles were pumped, sweat was pouring off his body and he was making incredible progress. He knew his foreman would be very pleased with his performance. But when his boss arrived, instead of congratulating the lumberjack for a job well done, the boss started ranting and raving. You see, although the lumberjack was breaking records and cutting more trees than anyone had ever cut before, he was in the wrong forest!

This analogy represents perfectly how many personal trainers go about seeking clients. They spend much time, money and effort in a particular area only to figure out later that they were in the wrong "forest."

You can be the best, most qualified personal trainer and still fail miserably if you do not have a game plan for attracting clients to your business. A short-term and long-term marketing plan will ensure you maximize exposure for your services and take your revenues to the next level.

Marketing is the way you tell people about your business. It's how you get your message out into the community so people know who you are, what you do and where you do it. It's very important that your message is clear, consistent and effective.

What Works Best for You?

Before you determine which clients you are trying to reach—and, consequently, what direction your business is going to take—you need to get away and do a little brainstorming. Go somewhere with very few distractions so you can figure out which path you should take—which forest you should be in. Fill out the worksheet below. What are your strengths and weaknesses, your likes and dislikes? Take a few minutes to write your lists. This exercise will help you set your direction.

Personal Strengths and Weaknesses

My strengths are:

Working with people
Organizing
Problem solving

My weaknesses are:

Not patient
Lack confidence with social media
Marketing

Likes and Dislikes

I like:

Meeting new people
Helping people
Rehabilitation
Triathlon coaching

I do not like:

Writing

Your Personal Strengths and Weaknesses

You might have a solid educational background that has prepared you to work with higher-risk clients, or perhaps you're an experienced athlete who can focus on sport-specific training. Or you may be aware that you are extremely impatient, which could mean you shouldn't work with postrehabilitation or medically compromised clients, who often progress at a much slower rate than healthy clients.

Your Likes and Dislikes

Perhaps you love working with older adults, clients with physical disabilities or high-achieving amateur athletes. Your likes will help determine your niche market. Being good at something isn't enough to set a direction. For example, what if you are a really good cleaner but hate cleaning? It would not be in your best interest to become a cleaner even though you are really good at it.

Learning more about yourself and your strengths and weaknesses will help you decide the type of clients you should concentrate on, and identify the services you (or trainers who work with you) are capable of offering. The clients you identify become your **target market**, and the services you offer are your **product**.

The best option is the one that allows your strengths and talents to shine and enables you to be happy in the career you've chosen. I truly believe that to last in this industry, you need to do what you love and are good at. Luckily, there are so many options in our industry that we can all enjoy incredible success while conducting our personal training businesses slightly differently. You see, I believe in the abundance theory, which means there is room at the top for all of us.

Understanding Yourself as a Business

Whether you hire other trainers, work alone or work for someone else, you are a business. And as a business you need to be crystal clear on what your product really is. Ask yourself the following questions to help clarify critical factors that will allow you to reach potential and current clients. Get a notepad and write the answers down, to keep your thoughts focused.

What is my product?

Of course, the final product you're selling is results—you're going to help clients look and feel better. But how are you going to accomplish this? Are you selling private personal training, group personal training, partner personal training, outdoor personal training, in-home personal training or a combination of all these?

Where will I train clients?

Club, personal training studio, clients' homes, outdoors? The location of your business has an impact on the clients you can reach and the service level you can offer. Location also affects the prices you are able to charge. Generally, in the larger metropolitan areas you can justify higher fees, whereas in smaller communities, lower fees better match lower household incomes.

How will clients inquire about my services?

By telephone, e-mail or fax? Through the front desk at the club? The right system will enable you to receive all your messages and respond immediately with a telephone call or brochure, or by whatever method you select. Decide whether you will need a pager, a cell phone, voice mail, an e-mail system and/or a fax machine.

How will clients pay for sessions?

Cash, credit card, check? When? Where? Make this process as easy and convenient as possible for clients. The ability to accept credit cards and automatic debit cards is a must. Talk to your bank about setting up a merchant teller account; or visit one of the Web-based companies that assist with this process for a fee. In a club setting, payments are often taken care of for you. But if you're an independent trainer in a club or studio setting, you'll have to set up a solid system.

How will I file client information/programs?

You've got to be organized. You can't be misplacing files or trying to conduct a session from memory because you forgot the file at home. Organization may mean a filing system in your car, at home or in an office at the gym. You'll want easy access to a photocopy machine so you can copy information and programs for clients. Also, start thinking about what types of client forms you'll need to perform your job professionally.

Can someone who wants to start a new business and needs a bank loan just walk into the bank and get the money? Absolutely not. The banker requires a detailed business plan. Why? To ensure the person requesting the loan has thought through his or her ideas clearly so there's less chance the business is going to fail. A plan helps reassure the banker that the money will be repaid. Being prepared to answer questions about your business is critical.

Unfortunately, I can't give you the "right" answer to every possible question because there are so many right answers. Do your homework, thoroughly examine the big picture and set up your products and markets to enable you to do something you love and do it well.

Location Logistics

If you are starting a business, it's important to be fully aware of the pros and cons of each venue so you can make wise choices. If you've already set up shop, you may need to reevaluate your situation.

Health clubs generally offer lots of equipment options and a built-in base of potential customers. Working in a health club is a great way to start your career as a trainer—you may find it difficult finding clients otherwise. On the other hand, members who already pay to access the club may not want to pay more for personal training, and you may have to deal with members who are disgruntled because they perceive you as "hogging" the equipment.

Many clubs no longer allow independent trainers within their facilities, instead requiring trainers to become employees, which often means a lower income. But on the bright side, working as an employee in a club setting provides a consistent source of income and some stability and security, as well as marketing and bookkeeping support. If you find a club that still welcomes independent contractors, you and the owner will decide how you'll pay for usage of the club space and equipment. Some clubs require a percentage of what the client pays (ranging from 20-70%). Other clubs charge a monthly rental fee or a per-client fee. Establish an arrangement that is win-win for you and the club so you can count on this being your home for the long term.

Clients' homes ensure privacy and require little overhead for you as the trainer, but may provide limited equipment, and you must remember to account for travel time. Plus, since no one sees you training your clients, you may find it takes more time to grow your business.

Personal training studios, which are popping up in metropolitan areas, have the advantages of privacy and a range of equipment, but require that clients travel to you. Some studios cater to the independent trainer while others require trainers to be employees. You may be thinking about opening your own studio. Overhead costs include rent, utilities, equipment and other miscellaneous expenses. If studio ownership is your goal, definitely hire a consultant and complete a detailed business plan to ensure you'll be able to generate enough revenue to cover your costs.

Before deciding where to conduct your business, I encourage you to shop around. You'll quickly learn that you have many options to succeed.

Plan to Succeed

Do you remember the story of Alice in *Alice's Adventures in Wonderland*? Alice asks the cat, "Would you tell me, please, which way I ought to go from here?" The cat responds, "That depends a good deal on where you want to get to." "I don't much care where," answers Alice. The cat replies, "Then it doesn't matter which way you go."

To get someplace, you've got to know where you're going. Sometimes, when personal trainers hire me to help them establish their careers, we hit a stumbling block right at the get-go. I ask, "In an ideal world, what would you like your personal training business to look like?" And they're dumbfounded. They can't answer me. They're really not sure. Well, then we have a problem, haven't we? How can I help them reach their goals if they're not sure what their goals are?

Start by making a list of the characteristics of your ideal personal training business. Would you own your own business? Where would you train? Would you open up your own personal training studio? Would you have multiple studios? How many trainers would you have working for you, or would you just work solo—or perhaps be an employee of a large, well-established health club? How many clients would you have? How much personal training revenue would you generate every year? How many hours per week would you train? Try to be as detailed as possible in your wish list. Get an 8 ½ × 11 sheet of paper and write out your wish list now.

Unfortunately, simply having a goal or vision won't cut it. You need a step-by-step, milepost-by-milepost plan. Some trainers I've worked with have an easy time coming up with their dream but when I ask them, "Okay, where do we go from here," they don't have a clue. They can see the big picture, but it's so overwhelming, they just don't know where to start.

Without a plan, you can easily lose sight of your goal, just as you can lose your way on a trip if you don't have a map. Your plan for going after your dream is important because, let's face it, this is a long trip and you want to enjoy the ride.

Don't be like Alice or the Canadian lumberjack. Figure out where you are and where you want to go before you start out.

5 trainers (20 clients each) 100 clients $2500/week or $8000/mo

Planning Worksheet

List at least 3 things you can do tomorrow to move you closer to your ultimate career goal.

Fix my website (Tune it up)

Train Kinesiologist

Use Facebook - Ask people to "like" EMF.

List at least 3 things you can do next week to move you closer to your ultimate career goal.

Shoot videos for Trainerize

Put videos up on YouTube

Write "e report" which is carrot for signing up for newsletter.

List at least 3 things you can do next month to move you closer to your ultimate career goal.

Put up posting for newsletter writer.

Host seminars. - collect peoples email address for newsletter

Shoot video for my home page

List at least 3 things you can do next year to move you closer to your ultimate career goal.

Join e women network.

Shoot 1 month bootcamp workout.

Save for new website

List at least 3 things you can do within the next 5 years to move you closer to your ultimate career goal.

Collect larger database of client's email address

Learn about franchising / branding

Congratulations! You have a plan. Feels great, doesn't it?

CHAPTER TWO
Who Are Your Clients?

If you can see the client through the client's eyes, you can sell the client what the client buys.

Now that you've inventoried your personal strengths and the goals for your business, it's time to apply them to the type of client you'll be most successful with. In business terms, it's time to decide upon your **niche market**, or the type of client you'll specialize in. Honing in on the type of client you want to attract to your business will make your marketing plan focused and successful. You won't be shooting in the dark. You'll still be able to appeal to a variety of clients, but you'll target your efforts at one or 2 key groups. The next few exercises will help you choose these groups.

First, look at your lists of likes and strengths. What types of clients fit your skills? What are their goals or special needs? How old are they? What's their gender? What's their income level? (Will you keep your prices lower to attract more people of a lower income level or will you cater to high-end clients?) To get you thinking, here are a few types of clients:

- beginning exercisers
- veteran exercisers who have experienced a plateau
- clients in rehabilitation from an injury or in cardiac postrehab
- recreational athletes trying to improve sports performance
- elite athletes
- young athletes
- kids
- overweight kids

- pre/postnatal or menopausal women
- clients with diabetes or osteoporosis
- overweight men and women
- baby boomers
- people over 60 years old
- bodybuilders
- business executives
- at-home mothers/wives

If you're not sure what type of client to focus on, statistics from the 1999 IDEA/ASD Personal Fitness Training Survey might help. According to this survey, 60% of personal training clients are women and 40% are men. The average age of clients is 37 years, and they are generally highly educated (48% college graduates) with upscale incomes ($75,000 average household income). Focusing your marketing initiatives on this type of client is a good place to start. If you already have clients, identify the type of client who seems drawn to you and the type of client who has had the most success working with you.

Target Market Worksheet

Type of client I would like to work with:

Middle aged professional women

Type of client who seems to be drawn to me:

Middle aged women.

Type of client I am most successful with:

Women. Rehabilitation client.
↳ not necessarily athletic

You can either continue to attract the type of client you already do well with (which is always easiest!) or look toward a market you have not yet attracted. You may find that the type of client you currently work with is also targeted by many other trainers, in which case the market may be saturated, requiring you to expand your focus. (You'll learn more about identifying the competitive marketplace in the next chapter.) Let's say that all your clients seem to be married women and you want to branch out. Well, an obvious group to target would be your present clients' husbands—most likely, they're already sold on how great you are!

Once you know who your clients or potential clients are, you can speak specifically to them in your marketing campaigns. But don't stop with the information gathered so far. If you really want to understand your clients and their buying patterns, you've got to collect more data.

Learn About Your Clients

You can analyze your target market by collecting information about your current clientele. Distribute a single-page, double-sided questionnaire to your clients asking about themselves. If you don't currently have clients, you can ask friends or family who fit the target market profile, and get information from public sources such as the chamber of commerce.

Asking your clients questions helps you gain a thorough understanding of the demographics and psychographics of your niche market. A **demographic analysis** provides information about a typical client's population characteristics, and profiles variables like age, sex, family status, occupation, income, expenditures on leisure, level of education, etc. A **psychographic analysis** reveals psychological information about lifestyle preference, self-image, personality type, readiness to exercise, motives for exercise, attitudes about health, moral values and opinions.

Following are the types of questions to ask. Please feel free to add any other areas you're interested in.

What is your age, gender, income level, marital status, education level, occupation?

If you discover that 80% of your clients are married, you may decide to aggressively promote partner training to attract your clients' spouses or partners. If you discover that 75% of your clients are lawyers, you may consider advertising in a directory or publication geared toward the legal profession. If you notice that 90% of your clients are women, you might begin marketing yourself as a trainer who specializes in women's issues.

Why did you purchase personal training?

If you learn that 90% of your clients want to lose body fat, you'll know to address this concern in your marketing materials.

How did you hear about me?

For example, if 90% of your clients heard about you from a friend or colleague, you'll know you should focus on establishing strong referral systems.

Why did you purchase personal training sessions with me instead of another trainer or organization?

If you determine that 80% of people purchased personal training with you because they perceived you have the greatest amount of knowledge, you'll continue to include information about your credentials on your personal dossier and regularly update clients on things you're learning through trade journals and conferences.

Why do you continue to do business with me?

If your clients tell you they continue doing business with you because you keep them motivated, you'll realize how important it is to maintain a strong accountability system, regularly follow up with clients and carefully track their adherence.

How far away do you live?

If 98% of your clients live within a 10-minute drive of your studio, you'd do well to focus direct-marketing efforts on the local zip/postal codes.

Which local newspaper do you read? Which sections? Which radio/TV stations do you listen to?

If the same percentage of clients read the local, community newspaper as the larger city newspaper, you can advertise to the right market for a lot less money. The same applies to radio stations.

Which events/activities do you participate in monthly?

If you discover that a majority of your clients golf or ski, you can establish cross-promotions and strategic alliances with golf centers and ski resorts.

Do you use e-mail?

If all your clients have access to e-mail, you may establish a marketing and customer service campaign that focuses on this affordable and user-friendly option.

A solid understanding of who your clients are allows you to focus all your marketing initiatives, which saves lots of time and money in the long run.

CHAPTER THREE
Know Your Competition

"You cannot discover new horizons unless you have the courage to lose sight of the shore."

Knowing the market(s) you will service is not enough. There are other trainers seeking these same clients. Defining your market means defining the businesses that are your competition, and figuring out how you will position yourself to differ from them. Remember, you don't need to have a "cutthroat" approach to succeed. In fact, if all personal training businesses worked together (as airline companies are starting to do by forming strategic alliances), we'd all reach new heights of success. Let's examine how you learn to truly understand your competition and use that understanding to help elevate your business.

I'd like you to start by writing down 10 shampoo brands. You heard me right. For example, one might be Finesse. (You can't use that one!) Give yourself one minute. Ready, go!

1. _____
2. _____
3. _____
4. _____
5. _____
6. _____
7. _____
8. _____
9. _____
10. _____

How'd you do?

Now, list 10 of your competitors. These could be fitness gyms, personal training studios or independent personal trainers. Again, give yourself one minute.

1. Fitness To Go
2. RJ Rehab
3. Innovative Fitness
4. Engineered Bodies
5. Recreation Centre?
6. _____
7. _____
8. _____
9. _____
10. _____

I imagine you performed a lot better listing your competitors than naming shampoo brands. Why? Because you've made it your business to know your competitors. And that's good! But do you really, really know your competitors? Do you completely understand their businesses? To do so, you've got to practice due diligence.

Go to your competitors' places of business. Check out the equipment, the clients and the staff. Pick up their brochures and promotional flyers. Check out how busy they are. Determine their niche market and atmosphere. Perhaps have a friend or colleague visit the business as a client to report on the experience from a client's perspective. You don't have to feel unethical or shady. Success in any business depends on understanding what's going on in the market.

Now identify the strengths and weaknesses of 7 of your competitors. You'll find a worksheet on the next page.

Do you notice any gaps in services provided? Has a particular market group been neglected? For example, you may notice that the majority of your competition is centered in residential communities and no one has tapped the downtown corporate market. Or you may notice that your competition is sufficiently servicing the baby boomer market, but no one is servicing clients above the age of 60. Or you may notice that no one is focusing on in-home training services. Examining your competition may help you focus on an area you'd enjoy pursuing.

Competitor Worksheet

Competitor	Strengths	Weaknesses
1. Fitness To Go	Professional Concise Marketing	Don't cater to women specifically or older population or injured.
2.		
3.		
4.		
5.		
6.		
7.		

Now ask yourself the following question, and write down your answers:

What can I offer that the competition can't or won't?

_____

_____

_____

CHAPTER FOUR

Pricing Your Services

"Starting out to make money is the greatest mistake in life. Do what you have a flair for doing, and if you are good enough at it money will come."

William Rootes

Before you can market your services, you have to identify exactly what they are and what they will cost. In personal training, the product you are selling is improved health and fitness. You must position yourself as the tool that provides the knowledge clients need to achieve their fitness goals. But you can package the knowledge you provide in a variety of ways. Offering different service packages enables you to offer a variety of prices.

There is no universal "right" way to establish your pricing. It is done differently by different businesses. There are guidelines, however, to ensure you stay on the right track:

- Prices must be high enough to cover your expenses and allow for a profit margin high enough to justify your time. Prepare a budget.

- Review the pricing structures of other personal training businesses in your area. Just to give you an idea, the IDEA/ASD 1999 Personal Fitness Training Survey reported that clients paid an average of $34 per session (27% paid under $25, 27% paid $25-$49, 13% paid $50-$74 and 5% paid above $75).

- Raise your prices once per year to account for inflation and a higher cost of living.

- Always collect fees up front. (Okay, collecting is different from pricing, but if you don't collect the money, your prices won't make any difference!)

PERSONAL TRAINING PACKAGES

Looking Good & Feeling Great!

Private Training Rates:

Number of sessions	Cost per session	Savings per session	Cost per package
50	$50.00	$6.00	$2500.00
35	$51.00	$5.00	$1785.00
20	$51.50	$4.50	$1030.00
15	$53.50	$2.50	$802.50
10	$54.00	$2.00	$540.00
5	$55.00	$1.00	$275.00
1	$56.00	N/A	$56.00

Partner Training Rates:

Number of sessions	Cost per session	Savings per session	Cost per package
50	$66/session $33/person	$15.00	$3300.00 $1650/person
35	$66.75/session $33.37/person	$14.63	$2336.25 $1168.12/person
20	$67.50/session $33.75/person	$14.25	$1350.00 $675.00/person
15	$68.25/session $34.12/person	$13.88	$1023.75 $511.87/person
10	$69/session $34.50/person	$13.50	$690.00 $345.00/person
5	$70.50/session $35.25/person	$12.75	$352.00 $176.25/person

At-Home Training Rates:

Number of sessions	Cost per session	Savings per session	Cost per package
50	$62.00	$4.00	$3100.00
35	$62.50	$3.50	$2185.50
20	$63.00	$3.00	$1260.00
15	$63.50	$2.50	$952.50
10	$64.00	$2.00	$640.00
5	$65.00	$1.00	$325.00
1	$66.00	N/A	$66.00

Full Fitness Assessment:
- $60.00
- A 1 hour thorough assessment evaluating your cardiovascular level, flexibility, muscular strength/endurance, blood pressure, RHR and body composition

Basic Fitness Assessment:
- $30.00
- A 30 minute basic assessment that will evaluate your blood pressure, RHR, body composition and flexibility

Ask About our Specialty Programs:
- Nutrition Counseling
- Group Fat Loss Programs
- "Knowledge is Power" Workshop Series
- Group Training
- Running Clinic
- Hiking Club
- Inline Skating Clinics

Northwest PERSONAL TRAINING & Fitness Education

Sample Pricing

You can use our price structure from NorthWest Personal Training & Fitness Education as a template. This structure offers packages that range from 5 to 50 sessions. Very few people will actually purchase the 50-session package—about one person a month, maybe, depending on the market. My experience is that most people purchase a package of between 10 and 20 sessions. People seem to like to purchase somewhere in the middle, between the high and low extremes. So, although very few people purchase the high-end package, it's a good idea to offer one just to have the upper extreme. When I first started training, my largest package was 10 sessions, and most people seemed to purchase 4 to 5 sessions; when I increased my largest package to 20 sessions, most people purchased 8 to 10; and when I increased the largest package to 50 sessions, more and more people purchased 15 to 20.

You'll notice that discounts are offered for multisession packages. According to the 1996 IDEA Personal Training Business Survey, 81% of trainers use this type of system. Packages encourage clients to commit to more sessions up front to get a better deal.

You could try a different approach by charging a monthly or weekly fee—for example, 3 sessions per week for $150 a week; 2 sessions per week for $120 a week; or one session per week for $70. This type of system is advantageous if you are set up with a merchant account because then you can debit clients' accounts every week or every month. Clients enjoy the convenience of this system.

Promotional Offers

You could complement your basic pricing structure with promotional offers throughout the year. The package I've been most successful with is the "Quick-Fix" program. Scott McLain initially developed this program at Westerville Athletic Club in Ohio. I tried it and it was so successful, I decided to repackage it so I could offer it yearly. The program I offer is generally as follows:

"Quick-Fix" Package Sample
3x each week with a personal trainer
7 weeks of focused, intense training
one-hour sessions ($\frac{1}{2}$ hour independent cardio and $\frac{1}{2}$ hour muscle conditioning)
$499

Notice that the client actually receives a half hour with her trainer. Let's say her appointment is scheduled at 9:00. She starts the cardio at 9:00 and the trainer meets her at 9:30. But she does get a one-hour workout 3 times per week. Within

7 weeks of adhering to this program, she will experience very significant results, which will improve the chance of her renewing with the trainer.

Even though the price may be very similar between this package and the 10-session package, the way the "Quick-Fix" program works makes it easy to convince people to commit to personal training. You can offer the program year-round and just change the name and the focus. For example, in November offer "Quick-Fix" as the "Countdown to the New Year" holiday package; in May offer the "Get Into Shape for Summer" package; in March offer the "Spring Training Camp" package; and in January offer the "Resolution Solution" package.

I'd much rather do this type of promotion than, for example, 3 sessions for $99, because short-term offers don't really give people a feel for what personal training is all about. However, this type of program does not work for in-home training, since you don't want to be driving all over the place for half-hour sessions.

Session Options

If you'd like to charge higher fees but don't think the market will bear it, try these creative approaches to making more money in less time.

Partner Training

Clients purchase partner training at 1½ times the normal personal training rate and then split the cost with one other person. For example, if the normal private training fee is $40 per hour, the partner training rate would be $60. Each of the 2 individuals pays only $30 per session. Clients purchase packages of, for example, 10 partner training sessions.

45-Minute Sessions

Restructure the length of your sessions. Instead of charging $50 for a one-hour session, charge $50 for a 45-minute session. This way you can still market your services for $50 per session. Be sure your client agreement clearly states that the sessions are only 45 minutes long.

30-Minute Private Resistance Training

One private training studio in Vancouver, British Columbia, developed a very creative and profitable way of organizing training sessions. Personal training is $40 per session, which is lower than the average fee in the local area. Clients arrive and complete an independent but supervised 30-minute cardio session in the studio. Thirty minutes later, the personal trainer takes them through a 30-minute resistance training workout. So in one hour, that trainer actually sees 2 clients, which translates into $80 revenue generated in one hour instead of $40. And the clients are still getting an hour's workout while enjoying lower fees.

CHAPTER FIVE

Profitable Personal Training Services

"To take a journey of a thousand miles, you have to begin with the first step;...the romantic description of the journey and the things the body sees on the way...are of no use unless you lift your foot and take the first step."

Vimala Thakar

If you've ever worked 8+ hours a day with clients scheduled back to back, you know how exhausting it can be. It's challenging to stay upbeat and positive all day and still have enough energy for your last client. The key to longevity in the fitness industry is living a balanced life, so you have to learn to work smarter, not harder.

The following programs allow you to make more money without having to work longer hours. These programs involve teaching a group of people in a sports clinic, lecture or multiple-client format. Group training allows you to add more services (your product lines) to your one-to-one exercise programs and offer more options for pricing. It also enables you to maximize client referrals and alliances with other businesses. That's good marketing!

Private training is still your "bread and butter." But I've seen personal training programs experience greater success and growth by offering various types of group training. And I'm not alone. The 2000 IDEA Fitness Programs Survey found that 54% of fitness facilities offer partner training, and 36% provide small group personal training. With this approach, everybody wins!

Trainers win because they earn more money in a given time slot. For example, Susan Cantwell, owner of The Fitness Specialists Personal Training, charges $80 per hour for a private session. For partner training she charges $65 per person, therefore earning $130 per hour. For a group of 3, she charges $55 per person, therefore making $165 per hour.

Clients win because they enjoy the cost-effectiveness of group training, not to mention the social environment that fosters the development of friendships. This in turn positively affects client adherence and consistency because no one wants to "drop out" on their friends.

And finally, group training satisfies most personal trainers' desire to make a difference in people's lives. Instead of appealing to only one person, you can make an impact on several people in the same amount of time.

Profits and Expenses

The largest expenses are wages for the trainers facilitating each of the programs. Most fitness facilities want at least 50% of the revenue generated as profit to the program. The other 50% can be used for trainer wages and miscellaneous expenses.

If you are a trainer pitching this idea to your club manager, don't start with a 50% revenue split. Propose a 30% share of the revenue to the club and then negotiate until you reach figures you're both happy with. Don't start any lower than a 30% club split. You are using the club's facilities and equipment, marketing to its members and, most likely, using its receptionists to oversee registration and payments.

Of course, if you own your own studio or operate these programs independent of a club, all the revenue minus expenses goes to you. But you should still establish a formula to determine how much of the money goes toward your hourly fees and how much is profit. This will help you determine how profitable a program is. For example, if 2 programs generate $3,000 each in revenue, but program A takes you 20 hours to facilitate and program B takes you 10 hours, it's clear that program B is much more profitable.

To find space for your group programs you may need to partner with another company, such as a retail fitness equipment store, which may want to charge you a rental fee. First, attempt to obtain free usage of the space. Many owners or managers, seeing the benefits of facilitating these types of programs within their businesses, will waive a rental fee. If you have to pay for space, include the rental fee in your expense calculations to ensure that the program is still profitable.

Advertising

I've always used very low-cost, grassroots, internal marketing for the group programs. You can design your own flyers on a computer and make photocopies. I am including some sample flyers that The Fitness Group and my company use.

Arms 101

Looking to improve your upper body strength? This program will provide you with upper body exercises guaranteed to give you shapely, toned arms. Don't go sleeveless without this program.

Thursdays 7:00-8:00pm
March 23 - April 27, 2006

TRACK WORKOUTS

Looking Good & Feeling Great!

Are you noticing that your speed just isn't the same?

As we get older, our muscle fibers will decrease in number and size - this loss is experienced predominantly in our fast-twitch fibers. This is why someone who is older moves much slower than when they were younger. The good news is research demonstrates that it's not aging that's the culprit, it's a lack of training. It's hard to be motivated to do speed sessions on your own! These group workouts will improve your fitness, help you lose body fat and will get you moving faster in all your recreational pursuits - your friends won't know what's got into you!

Thursdays 6:00pm

The First Tee

Personal Training Lecture

Studies have proven that muscular conditioni balance and flexibility training improve clubh speed and lead to a more powerful golf sw Learn warm-up, stretching and strengthe exercises that get you in top shape for the

Thursday 7:30-9:0
January 27, 20

Costs: S

Instructor:
Andrea Leupold, Personal Trai

See Front Desk to Reg

TRAINING CAMP

Looking Good & Feeling Great!

Do you want to get into the best shape of your life?

Join Sherri McMillan,
Author of *"Go For Fit - The Winning Way to Fat Loss"* &
IDEA International Personal Trainer of the Year Award winner
for:

- Speed, power and agility drills
- Interval training
- Muscle-conditioning
- Flexibility training
- Fat loss and Cardio-conditioning

Cost of $199 includes:
8 weeks of Weekly Group Training Workouts
Tuesday mornings 6:30-8:00am
September 12-October 31, 2000
Maximum 10 people so register early
(Non-members pay an additional $40 fee)

This weekly morning workout is not for the timid.
Be prepared to sweat!

Register at the Front Desk or contact 360.574.7292 for details.

Northwest PERSONAL TRAINING *& Fitness Education*

In a gym, post flyers on cardio machines, in washrooms and at all other available locations. That's generally all you need to do. Outside a fitness facility, ask other companies to post your flyers within their organizations, or rely on word of mouth. The key is to allow yourself enough time to thoroughly market your programs. My goal is to have all flyers posted or mailed at least 1 ½ months prior to the beginning of the program.

No matter which personal training program you offer, you'll find that after about a year, it will lose its novelty, and registration will start to drop. This is why you should restructure and repackage all your programs every year. For example, the training camp, ski and boarding camps, and golf conditioning programs are basically all the same type of program structure with a different focus. The group fat-loss program could be renamed to, say, "Outsmart Your Fat Cells." Remember that if a certain type of program doesn't work for you, it doesn't mean that no program will work for you. You really have to understand your clients and their needs and be ready to try something else.

Group Training Pointers

I've found that many participants in a group training program will purchase a few private sessions to customize their programs. You can include a special offer with all group training programs to encourage this. For example, on the first day give all the registrants a flyer that promotes 5 private sessions for the price of 4. With these types of offers, group training becomes a feeder into private training revenues.

Use the knowledge of your clients that you've gained through working with them and studying their questionnaires to pick one or 2 group programs you think will be very successful. Then spend all your time and energy promoting these programs. When you determine which types of programs work best for your organization, expand on them. In your marketing plan for the year, balance out when you offer each program. You don't want to offer too many at the same time because they will compete against each other.

Keep in mind that group training hasn't worked for everyone. Some clubs have experienced poor response from clients for some programs. In the traditional health club, most members appreciate having the choice of registering or not registering for any of the programs. Think about what most members are getting for their monthly membership fee—use of equipment and fitness classes. Charging extra for group programs helps you cover the costs without significantly raising membership fees! We undervalue our services way too often. Sometimes you have to try a couple of ideas before you find something that works for your clientele.

Each of these program models has a specific focus, design and package. Note that some of the programs are packaged so each participant receives a private training session before the program begins to establish goals, and after the program finishes to reassess. Clients enroll for a specific time, for example, Saturday mornings at 9:00 AM from May 1 to June 30. Some programs stay indoors, and equipment use ranges from minimal to extensive; other programs take clients outdoors. The key is to be creative!

Large Group Training (10-12 Clients)

This is an economical route for the client who wants regular motivation and education. Because clients split the costs among 10 to 12 people, they enroll in the program at a fraction of the cost of private or small group training. Yet each person receives more attention than if he attended a group exercise-to-music class.

The format is similar to a muscle-conditioning group workout or a circuit class. Bring an educational handout to each session and ask each participant to sign in and record how he met his fitness goals that week.

Option 1:
10-12 clients/1 trainer
2 private sessions per client (1 pre- & 1 postgroup)
8 weeks group training
One 1-hour group workout per week
Cost: $170 per person
Expenses: Wages & promotional flyers

This option works well for a muscle-conditioning format. You could call the program "Muscle," "Women and Weights," "Fight Bone Loss With Muscle," "Muscle—the Magic Pill to Reverse Aging" or "Fit After 40." Or you could promote a children's, teen or pre-/postnatal program.

Option 2:
10-12 clients/1 trainer
No private sessions
10 weeks group training
One 1 ½ -hour group workout per week
Cost: $150 per person
Expenses: Wages & promotional flyers

To keep costs down, private sessions are not offered. This type of protocol lends itself well to programs that are athletic and sport specific—for example, any type of boxing or kicking camp, boot camp, sports conditioning program, athletic drills, ski and skiboarding preparation, golf conditioning or tennis conditioning.

Option 3:
10-12 clients/1 trainer
No private sessions
6 weeks group training
One 1-hour group interactive session per week
Cost: $100 per person
Expenses: Wages & promotional flyers

For this option, a 101 series works really well, for example, "Abdominals 101," "Legs 101," "Arms 101" or "Back 101." Over the 6-week period, you teach clients everything about a particular body part.

Small Group Training (3-4 Clients)

This size group works well for resistance training, cardio training or specialized training (golf or tennis conditioning, athletic conditioning, circuit training). You can offer the small group as a course with a preassigned schedule so clients can enroll in a slot that works for them, or accommodate the time request of 3 to 4 friends who arrange to be trained at a specified time.

Option 1:
3-4 clients/1 trainer
Cost: 3 people for $26 per person; or 4 people for $20 per person
Expenses: Wages & promotional flyers

With this option, clients can purchase packages of, say, 10 or more sessions. Encourage each client to invest in a few private sessions.

Option 2:
3-4 clients/1 trainer
3 private training sessions per client (2 pre- & 1 postgroup)
8 weeks group training (1-hour workouts)
Cost: $295 per person
Expenses: Wages & promotional flyers

Clients register for a particular time slot and schedule. While 4 clients are required to make the program very profitable, it can function with only 3 registrants. If only 2 people register, cancel the course and encourage the registrants to participate in partner training.

Running Clinic, Walking Clinic and Hiking Club

I have started a number of running programs throughout the years, and all continue to regularly attract 60 or more people per session. I offer a running clinic 3 times per year, starting in January, May and September. The clinics generally last 12 weeks, and each week the participants learn a different way to train (steady state, track workouts, fartlek, interval training, hills and so forth).

Sports clinics and clubs provide a great opportunity for you to align yourself with a local fitness clothing and footwear retailer. Start and finish at the store. Since the store owners enjoy many benefits from offering this type of program, they want to see it succeed. It's a value-added service for their customers. If you get 20 people enrolled, 20 people will come to the store weekly. These people will most likely need to purchase fitness clothing and footwear—and will probably make their purchases at the host store. You can negotiate to send promotional flyers to all the store's customers, place flyers in customers' shopping bags and post flyers and bulletins around the store.

Option 1:
60+ registrants
1 coordinator/5-10 group leaders
1 ½ - to 2-hour sessions
12-week program
Cost: $99 per person
Expenses: Volunteers' gifts, promotional flyers, running logs & year-end party

Running groups range in level from a run-walk to a 7-minute-mile pace. To facilitate the required pace, I recruit a number of volunteers who are runners, fitness leaders or very motivating people. I budget into my expenses a gift for each of my volunteers (pair of Nike shoes, Nike watch, vest or other article of clothing).

The clinic workouts look something like this:

5 minutes: Introductions & workout description

10 minutes: Group warm-up walk & dynamic range of motion exercises

25-60 minutes: Workout in pace groups

5 minutes: Cool-down walk

10-20 minutes: Final stretch & educational health talk

I try to recruit sponsors like Nike, PowerBar and local businesses so I can offer regular door prizes to the group and purchase running logs and the volunteers' gifts at below-wholesale prices. You might even get a local pub to sponsor the clinic and get your clinic-end party at almost no cost.

This concept also lends itself well to a hiking club. I like to include an educational lecture to review safety procedures and protocol before the hikes. Dates and times of all the hikes are prescheduled.

Option 2:

25 registrants maximum
1 coordinator/3 group leaders
3+-hour hikes
5-6 hikes
Cost: $125 per person
Expenses: Volunteers' gifts, promotional flyers & year-end party

Perhaps you could start a beach volleyball club, a cross-country ski clinic, a tennis program, a triathlon training clinic, a mountain biking program, a cycling club or an indoor rock-climbing club. The sky is the limit.

Health and Fitness Lectures

Health and fitness lectures offer a wonderful opportunity to educate your clients. Encouraging clients to bring their friends, family members and coworkers offers the opportunity to gain exposure for your services. After all, you've got an audience of people who want to know more about the topic you're presenting. It becomes very easy to get those people excited about your services and interested in purchasing private or group training sessions.

There are many opportunities to present health lectures at corporate facilities, fitness facilities or local businesses. When proposing a health and fitness lecture to a business owner or manager, use the same approach you would to develop a strategic alliance. (For more information see chapter 9.) If you have, or want to develop, good speaking skills, these types of lectures can definitely help you grow your business.

The most popular topics tend to be anything about fat loss or nutrition. Lectures that address the best ways to condition abdominals or develop a healthy back also do very well. You can advertise lectures to specific populations, such as baby boomers, women with osteoporosis, menopausal women, triathletes, vegetarians, gardeners or teenage athletes. You could offer cooking classes or recipe lectures to teach people "quick 'n' easy" healthy meals.

Some trainers offer free lectures to clients as an extra, value-added service. In my experience, when you charge a nominal fee of $8 to $20 per lecture, more people register. It's almost as if they think if it's free, it must not be that good. However, other people who offer free seminars have done very well with this approach. If you charge for your lecture and get an average of 25 registrants, the revenue will help offset the time involved with preparing for the talk. Generally, you can expect to spend double to quadruple the length of the lecture on preparation time (1-hour lecture = 2 to 4 hours preparation), so it's nice to enjoy some level of financial compensation.

Group Fat-Loss Lectures (10-12 Clients)

This program has been a huge winner from both a financial and a client success perspective. Each registrant receives a fitness assessment to establish baseline fitness and body composition measurements. An option is for each client to keep a 3-day food record, which is analyzed by a nutritionist. Each registrant receives a workbook that includes nutrition and activity logs, educational information, homework assignments and more.

10-12 clients/1 trainer
Pre- & postgroup fitness assessment (includes basic body composition
 analysis & Polaroid shots)
Nutritional analysis
8-week program
1-hour lecture
Cost: $295 per person
Expenses: Wages, promotional flyers, manuals & Polaroid shots

Good times to offer this program are January, April, May and October. The workbook I use is the one I wrote, called *Go For Fit, The Winning Way to Fat Loss*. I wrote this workbook for the specific purpose of facilitating group fat-loss programs. The first week of the program I assign partners who will review each other's daily activity and diet logs and provide support for each other. I establish the expectations and guidelines for the program and assign reading material for each week.

In the following weeks I cover material ranging from designing a fat-loss exercise or nutrition program to portion control, to the psychology of fat loss and body image. Participants record a synopsis of each week so I know how they are doing in relation to their goals. At the end of 8 weeks, we perform another fitness assessment to measure progress.

Note that this program is completely lecture format. For cost-effectiveness, there are no workouts. Clients are given workout guidelines and assigned the responsibility of adhering to those guidelines. This is another great opportunity for a trainer to suggest a few private sessions.

The one-hour format would generally follow these time frames:

20 minutes: Partner review of previous week's nutrition & exercise logs, completion of weekly synopsis

20 minutes: Trainer lecture on a topic relating to fat loss, such as exercise programming, nutrition guidelines, body image, psychology of fat loss or behavioral change

20 minutes: Question, answer & discussion period

Here's some of the feedback I've received from this program, taken directly from evaluation sheets:

- *"I received motivation, support and accountability to the group."*
- *"I loved all the informational articles and homework."*
- *"I learned painless things I could do to decrease the amount of calories I eat each day."*
- *"I learned that a 20-minute workout was better than no workout."*
- *"I feel much healthier and in control of my life. The extra energy is a plus for my kids and husband. I have lost 15 pounds—better yet, I'm fitting into all the clothes in my closet, an economic plus."*
- *"I appreciate the 80/20 approach."*
- *"I have developed a strong feeling of self worth—I'm worth it!"*

As you can see, the program is not only about fat loss. Our group discussions are so much more meaningful than information that focuses only on the pursuit of a "perfect body."

If you're not in a club setting, you could approach a local spa owner about offering an 8-week group fat-loss program within the spa. Most people who attend spas are the same type who would consider consulting with a personal trainer, so it's a natural fit. You can offer the spa a percentage of fees or pay a rental fee for usage of its space and the right to market to its customers. Host the program after regular spa hours so space is not an issue. The spa also wins because it is providing a service to its customers that it could not offer without you.

Program Resources

Go For Fit, The Winning Way to Fat Loss (RainCoast Publishing) can be purchased by visiting the publisher at www.raincoast.com or by e-mailing me at sherri@NWPersonalTraining.com.

GET REAL: A Personal Guide to Real-Life Weight Management is a weight loss book and program that IDEA offers. www.ideafit.com

CHAPTER SIX

What Is Your Marketing Message?

**You've got to know what you're doing/You've got to know you know
what you're doing/You've got to be known for what you know!**

I had braces all through high school. Imagine wearing braces through those awkward years when the opinion of your peers was so important to your feelings of self-worth! As I neared the end of high school, I scheduled an appointment with my orthodontist and asked him to remove my braces. He said, "No, your teeth are not ready yet!" And I said, "I don't care. I want the braces off. My teeth are straight enough. I'm not going to my prom and graduation with braces." So I forced him to remove the braces prematurely.

You see, most people hate wearing braces. They can't wait until the day they are removed. Then why do people wear braces? Because they want straight teeth. They are willing to go through the pain of wearing braces so they can get straight teeth. Similarly, do you really think most people want personal trainers? No way! They want results. They want to look and feel good, and a personal trainer is a way to help them get what they want. It's critical in marketing materials to focus, not on yourself or the business, but on the results a client will achieve from working with you on a regular basis.

You'll never see an orthodontist selling the look of braces. "Oh, these braces are wonderful. The steel is so pretty. You'll just light up a room." An orthodontist sells braces by showing patients what their teeth will look like once the braces come off. Remember to sell the straight teeth (results), not the braces (yourself). Of course, your clients will want to be sure that you are qualified and know what you're doing. But initially, connect with clients by showing them how you can help them rather than focusing on how great you are.

Keep this in mind. People will buy any product or invest in any service that will help them:

- Feel good.
- Look good, look sexy, feel attractive.
- Be healthier.
- Gain knowledge.
- Have fun.
- Save time.
- Be more comfortable.
- Feel important.
- Live longer.
- Save money.
- Achieve convenience.

Most important, people will buy when they want to change something about their present situation. You pinpointed one or more niche markets to target in chapter 2. Now determine what your particular niche market wants to change, and address this in all your marketing materials.

Which "triggering" events may have happened in your target clients' lives to make them want or need your services? Maybe your target market is starting to experience the effects of menopause—in your materials, address the specific needs of people in this life stage. Maybe your market is starting to get older—address the needs of an aging clientele. Or perhaps you want to market to pre-/postnatal clients—explain how you'll meet their unique concerns.

Remember this very wise marketing strategy: "If you see through the client's eyes, you can sell what the client buys." Understand your clients so you can talk directly to them.

Why You?

It is a good idea to be able to confidently and eloquently answer the following questions:

Why hire a personal trainer?
I'm sure you could easily list the benefits of working with you: You provide efficiency and effectiveness so clients don't waste any time in the gym. You design a safe program to minimize injury. You provide inspiration and accountability. You regularly introduce variety and progression. Your programs are fun and interesting.

You help clients develop self-worth and self-confidence. You regularly teach them new and interesting exercises using various exercise tools. You educate them. You foster a social environment.

These are all important benefits you must be able to eloquently discuss with clients. But even more important is being able to speak your clients' language. According to the 1998 IDEA Personal Training Survey, here's why clients consult with a personal trainer:

- 84% want to improve their muscle tone and body shape.
- 78% want to manage their weight.
- 72% want to improve their exercise adherence.
- 70% want to develop their muscular strength and flexibility.
- 65% want to improve their overall lifestyle.
- 37% want to recover from an injury or illness.
- 32% want to satisfy social needs.

It's important for you to clearly demonstrate that you can help people achieve these goals.

Why hire *you* as a personal trainer?

Although you don't want to focus on yourself when marketing your services, potential clients do want to know you are a top-notch trainer. Be able to verbalize the distinguishing characteristics that set you apart from other trainers. (You listed your strengths in chapter 1.)

Testimonials

Since you are in the fitness industry, you are probably familiar with the Tae-Bo™ craze. And you probably realize that forms of Tae-Bo have been around for years. Fitness gyms around the world have been offering group fitness classes that incorporate kicking and boxing for a very long time. So why the popularity of Tae-Bo? Solid marketing is the answer! If you watch a Tae-Bo infomercial, you'll quickly notice that a great majority of its content focuses on testimonials—people expressing how Tae-Bo has changed their lives.

Testimonials use phrases such as, "Since I've started using XYZ, I feel better than I ever have in my whole life," or "I've lost so much weight since starting XYZ, and I love all the attention I'm getting" or "I've tried so many diets and other programs before and nothing's ever worked—XYZ was the first program that actually got me the results I wanted."

Testimonials work. People like to know that others like themselves tried the service or product and got results. It makes them feel, "Hey, if they can do it, maybe I can too!" Use testimonials and success stories of real-life clients in all your promotional materials. Have clients list the benefits they've achieved, and the positive effects on their lives. On a side note, be sure to get their approval before using their quotes.

The Power of Words

Since most personal training businesses use brochures and other print marketing materials, it's important to recognize that what you put down on paper may positively or negatively affect your business.

Some words are more powerful than others and will more easily represent your image. Marketing gurus have outlined a number of words that, when used in marketing materials, encourage people to buy. When creating your marketing brochure and materials, attempt to use some of these power words.

Words to use in a headline:
- Announcing
- At last
- How to
- How
- Why
- Which
- New
- Now
- Who else
- Wanted
- This
- Advice

Words to use in supporting text:
- Now
- Discovery
- Health
- Sensational
- Improvement
- Compare
- New
- Proven
- You
- Introducing
- The truth about
- Miracle
- Quick
- It's here
- Announcing
- Challenged
- Startling
- Offer
- Wanted
- Money
- Remarkable
- Last chance
- Revolutionary
- Important development
- Guarantee
- Safety
- Results
- Easy
- Love
- Magic
- Save

Writing the Message

Alvin Eicoff, a well-regarded marketing guru, has a formula for writing promotional text.

1. State the problem.

2. Explain the solution.

3. Demonstrate how your specific service best provides the solution.

These 3 things must be accomplished in a clear, clever and concise way. Most marketing experts suggest using as little text as possible to avoid confusing the buyer's eyes. A few successful businesses have done just that.

For example, one of McDonald's restaurants' positioning statements is, "Have you had your break today?" In this quick question, the company fulfills Eicoff's rules. The problem is that people are rushing from appointment to appointment and deadline to deadline. The solution is to slow down, stop and take a well-deserved break. Finally, McDonald's suggests that its restaurants provide the food, convenience and environment that offer the break people need. In that one question, McDonald's has spoken its message. We can learn from the McDonald's marketing geniuses and use text such as, "Have you had your workout today?"

Or consider the LensCrafters message, "Glasses in less than an hour." This phrase suggests the problem: People are very busy and don't have a lot of time to waste. The solution is to get their glasses in less than an hour. And, of course, LensCrafters promises to achieve that. We can learn from the talent at LensCrafters and imagine a personal training headline that suggests, "Feel good in less than an hour," or "Looking and feeling good in less than an hour."

I encourage you to pay more attention to TV commercials and print ads. I think you can learn a lot from the way big businesses market their products and services. Remember, they have a huge budget and a staff of experts. It's easier to learn from them than to try to do it all on your own without access to the same money or talent.

You can use the brochure from NorthWest Personal Training & Fitness Education as a template. We had the assistance of a trained marketing consultant and graphic artist and we believe the brochure accomplishes what we had in mind. In chapter 7, you'll learn more about the mechanics of putting together a brochure. For now, read the copy in our brochure. It concentrates on attracting the baby boomer market. The brochure is client focused. It has a neat and attractive design and layout. (It's difficult to portray the color and style in this book, but take my word for it—it looks good!) It contains a call to action, motivating and inspiring words, and photos and testimonials. We have received many compliments on our brochure, and it is one we will keep for an indefinite period of time.

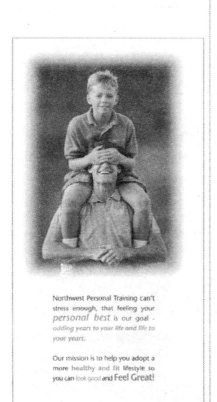

Northwest Personal Training can't stress enough, that feeling your *personal best* is our goal - adding years to your life and life to your years.

Our mission is to help you adopt a more healthy and fit lifestyle so you can look good and Feel Great!

We've come to realize that with all clients, it is not a matter of capacity or ability, it's a matter of getting them so **emotionally excited** about their fitness goals that no matter what other responsibilities or obstacles surface, they maintain their program.

We believe in getting our clients involved in **active adventures** and often take them hiking, *cycling*, indoor rock-climbing, inline skating or kayaking or we may play a game of pick-up basketball, or go for a run.

Your personal trainer will make exercise **fun**, enjoyable and interesting.

Looking good and **feeling great** is what our clients want.

At Northwest Personal Training, we know we can't treat everyone the same. **Your needs**, interests, goals and fitness levels are all different. However, we want everyone to **enjoy life** to the fullest by being able to pursue *whatever they desire*.

Being fit and healthy allows you to participate in whatever **your interest** may be, even if that means running along side your child as (s)he learns how to ride their new bike. NW personal trainers will create an exercise program that is custom-designed and **perfect for you.**

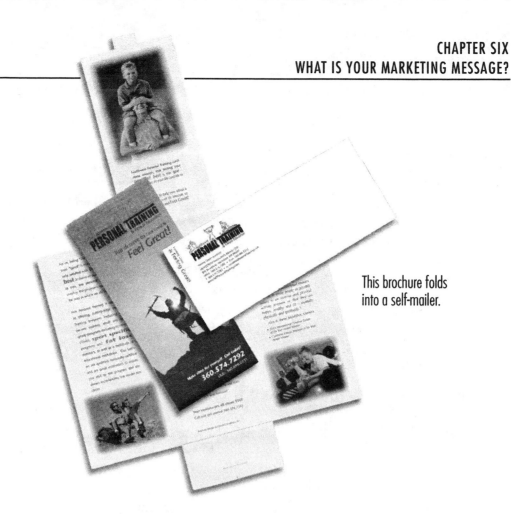

This brochure folds
into a self-mailer.

For us, being "OK" or "average" or even "good" is not enough. We are only satisfied with **being the best** in terms of quality of service to you, the personal trainers we employ, the programs operated and the way in which we do business.

NW Personal Training is dedicated to offering, cutting-edge Personal Training programs including one-on-one training, small and large group programs including *running clinics*, **sport specific** programs and **fat loss** seminars, as well as a multitude of educational workshops. Our trainers are qualified, nationally certified and are great motivators to ensure you stick to the program and are always experiencing the results you desire.

One size does not fit all!
You can exercise as often as you like with your trainer or as little as once every 6-8 weeks so your trainer can make a few adjustments to your program and help you stay on track.

Take Control of Your Life!
Personal Training gets results and that's why anyone can benefit from this personal attention! *Make an investment that will last a lifetime.* Personal Training is no longer reserved for Hollywood stars and the "rich and famous!"

Your sessions are all about YOU!
Call and get started 360.574.7292

Brochure Design by Deane's Graphics, Inc.

"Since I've worked with my personal trainer, I have lost 27 pounds, reduced my clothing by 3 sizes, and increased my muscle mass so that a recent test showed me to have muscle mass at 125% of normal for my age. I am now wearing clothes I haven't worn in 20 years."

"I felt extremely comfortable working with my personal trainer. He was knowledgeable, and an expert in his skills. I would recommend him to anyone serious about fitness!"

"It is our vision as personal trainers to assist as many people as possible adhere to an exercise and physical activity program so that they are happy, healthy and fit – mentally, physically and spiritually."

Alex & Sherri McMillan, Owners

- *IDEA International Personal Trainer of the Year Award Winner*
- *CanFitPro Fitness Presenter of the Year Award Winner*

Do Your Homework

Try to come up with a number of positioning statements similar to the ones listed above that you could use in a brochure or flyer. Spend an hour or more brainstorming and just write ideas on paper without evaluating them. Maybe get a few friends involved. The more creative minds involved, the better!

Once you have the headline or statement, start to write the supporting text using power words to address the concerns of your target market. Remember to answer the questions what, where, who, how and why. Refer to brochures from other personal training businesses for ideas.

Business Tools Become Messages

Your business will have a vision and a mission statement, values, a motto and a code of ethics. These statements of your business beliefs help to ground and focus your business in its direction. They are also excellent ways to convey your message to current and potential clients. Include the statements on the back of your business cards, the top of programming cards and the back of client birthday cards. Frame your code of ethics and values and hang them in your office or studio. Use these statements in your marketing materials and newsletters.

I am including a copy of the form we give to all our clients when they first consult with us. This form gives clients a clear picture of our mission, vision, motto and purpose as a company and as personal trainers. It instantly demonstrates that we've got our act together and are serious about what we do. This makes it easier for us to convince our clients that we can help them and also allows us to justify higher fees.

Vision and Mission Statement

Be clear and concise. State your mission in less than a paragraph. For example, at NorthWest Personal Training & Fitness Education, our vision is: "A personalized fitness program for everyone." Our mission statement is: "To help our clients adopt a more healthy and fit lifestyle so they look and feel better."

Other examples of mission statements:

- To provide a one-stop mind-body-spirit personal training experience for everyone.

- To offer affordable, high-quality personal training services to the general public.

- To help menopausal women achieve a healthy, balanced lifestyle.

- To assist other health professionals in rehabilitating people suffering from various physical injuries.

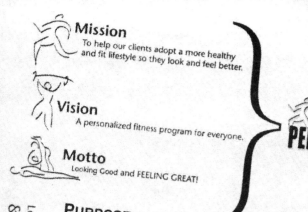

Mission
To help our clients adopt a more healthy and fit lifestyle so they look and feel better.

Vision
A personalized fitness program for everyone.

Motto
Looking Good and FEELING GREAT!

Looking Good & Feeling Great!

PURPOSE

As Personal Trainers, we must be able:

- To provide our clients with the knowledge, skills, guidance, support, motivation and educational resources that will allow them to explore their own fitness potential, as well as, enhance the quality of their lives now and ongoing.
- To offer safe programs, as well as, provide our clients with the knowledge, skills and exercise repertoire so that they can modify their exercise programs by themselves when needed.
- To develop fun, effective and efficient exercise programs that offer variety and meet the specific needs of our clients.
- To incorporate a holistic approach to health and fitness that encompasses cardiovascular fitness, muscular strength and endurance, flexibility, nutrition, stress and lifestyle considerations.
- To act as an aid in the rehabilitation of clients experiencing pain and injury.
- To network with the appropriate health and fitness professionals regarding the care of a client and incorporate recommendations as needed.
- To establish a warm, receptive and non-intimidating environment that facilitates and enhances the learning process.

As a Personal Training Department, we must be able:

- To express ourselves as a confident, competent and committed team of personal trainers whose primary focus is to enhance the quality of life and vitality of our clients.
- To remain certified and updated on all current research and fitness trends.
- To uphold professional integrity through our conduct, appearance and respect for our clientele, other personal trainers, and other fitness professionals and organizations within the industry.
- To share our knowledge, skills and insight with each other in order to enhance the department and our own image.

VALUES

Looking Good & Feeling Great!

1. PERSONAL TRAINERS

At NorthWest Personal Training and Fitness Education we realize that our business is only as good as our Trainers. So we only recruit and hire *the best*. We know that our clients want their personal trainer to exhibit the same qualities as any provider of any professional service, say, a lawyer, accountant or physician - a high degree of knowledge in their field, demonstrated expertise, plus a personality that's compatible with theirs. Here's a list of the attributes we look for and that you can expect from your NorthWest Personal Trainer:

a. Educated

Fitness information is always changing and that's why you need a company who values education and is committed to staying on the *cutting edge*. At NorthWest Personal Training, we understand that the minute a Personal Trainer stops learning, they cease to be a teacher. We have to keep learning so we will always be able to offer something new to our clients.

All of our trainers are certified through a nationally recognized association, attend regular fitness conferences, workshops and meetings and subscribe to a number of fitness trade journals. We also network with a variety of health professionals, massage therapists, and chiropractors. We physicians, nutritionists, physiotherapists, massage therapists, and chiropractors. We will know the answers to your questions and if we don't, we'll know where to find them.

b. Exceptional Teaching Abilities

At NorthWest we strive to teach you something *new* every single session. You may learn a new fitness fact, a new exercise or how to use a new piece of exercise equipment. Your trainer will provide you with regular fitness education articles. One thing for sure - there is no stopping to the extent of information you will receive from your personal trainer.

c. Desire to Help and Contribute

We only hire personal trainers who truly want to see people *succeed*. Our trainers get a great deal of personal satisfaction from knowing that they've played a role in helping their clients make positive changes to their lives. Our trainers really care. Expect your Personal Trainer to show up for sessions on time and prepared, expect to get regular motivational phone calls, and expect your trainers to put a lot of effort into designing your personalized fitness program...we strive to *exceed* our customers' expectations.

d. Strong Communication Skills

God gave us two ears and one mouth for a reason. To be a good communicator, you have got to be a good listener. Our Personal Trainers have been taught to listen to their clients so you can guarantee that your *needs* will be heard.

e. Honest

Our Personal Trainers will only act in your best interest. We are not here to just sell you a Personal Training package - we want to *service* your needs. It's as important to us as it is to you that you get the results you want. Any recommendations we make will be based on scientific research taking into account your interests, needs and goals.

---

f. Respectful

We understand the magnitude [...] can be assured that any infor[...]

g. Ability to Motivate

The sad fact is seven out of 10 [...] out within a few months. If you [...] may not be with you- it may be [...] too quickly without any planning [...]

We've come to realize that with [...] matter of getting them so *emotion*[...] what other responsibilities or obsta[...] at NorthWest, our Personal Trainer[...] the right types of systems and progra[...] **4-step process** that sets up a founda[...] adhere to their fitness program. Your [...] help you get internally motivated.

h. Able to Progress

At NorthWest, we know we can't treat al[...] generic fitness program from your Perso[...] fitness level and muscular imbalances w[...] designed. You will get an exercise progra[...] you! And your trainer will also know how t[...] starts to get fitter and stronger, your trainer [...] always experiencing great results.

i. Able to Inspire

Most people are inspired to do something by [...] thinking "Hey, if they can do it, so can I!" So [...] definitely "walk our talk" and lead by example. [...] adventures or events and often take them hikin[...] skating or kayaking. Your trainer may play bea[...] up basketball with you. Your trainer will make [...]

j. Projects a Positive, Upbeat, Energetic Atti[...]

We only hire Personal Trainers that people like to [...] definitely look for trainers who are educated, experi[...] but we also recognize that these skills without a [...] good *attitude* is a prerequisite before we will hire a[...]

k. Supportive

Of course, our clients need accountability. That's why [...] stick to the program. But there will be times when you [...] understand and you can be assured that your trainer w[...] always count on their *unconditional support*.

l. Professional

We are professionals at NorthWest Personal Training an[...] ways to *improve*. We will regularly ask you for your feed[...] ensure that we are satisfying your needs.

[...]elp clients achieve their goals. This means [...]s and giving them the tools, resources, and [...]chieving their goals.

[...] NorthWest Personal Training and Fitness [...]he industry's lowest dropout rates. [...]e-training program is mandatory for all

[...]ly including activities such as Sea [...]rding Trips, Horseback Riding, Running [...] Hood to Coast relay team. [...]thers will be scheduled regularly. [...]d monthly Personal Training meetings, [...]ervice component. [...]West Personal Training clients that will [...]apes, audiotapes, and magazines. [...]on bulletin boards and in company

[...]e best in the industry and will be

[...] new Personal Trainers to [...] values and practices. [...]t and opinions that affect [...]fore any decisions are made. [...]t for staff.

[...]ion s committed to offering [...]ram including one-on-one [...] educational lectures.

[...]d available for clients or

[...]al image. [...]ill have no hidden costs

[...]d upon and printed, [...]otiable to ensure a

[...]d business partners.

NorthWest PERSONAL TRAINING & Fitness Education

Motto

Our business is focused on feeling great, so our motto says: "Looking good and feeling great."

Our materials emphasize the "feeling great" with a larger font size and prominent placement.

Other motto examples:

- 100% customer satisfaction.
- Most affordable personal training services.

Values

Which values are most important to you? Do you value high-quality equipment and amenities, education, high-end training services, cleanliness, ethical business practices and procedures, customer service, cutting-edge programming, profitability, community involvement, happy and satisfied staff, client retention, or alliances with local businesses that share a common vision and values? I am including a copy of the value statements our business was founded on. Again, this is something we distribute to new clients that instantly shows them we are serious about our business, not just going through the motions.

Code of Ethics

IDEA Health & Fitness Association has established a code of ethics for the personal training industry that you can use or model. Frame a copy and post it in your office or studio. You can access it by visiting IDEA's Web site at www.ideafit.com.

Using Your Marketing Message

The marketing message you use will establish your business in your community and provide potential clients with a "flavor" of what you or your company can offer. What's most important is that the message you send is correct and consistent. If you say one thing but do another, your clients will be confused. So think your message through carefully; then you can rest assured that your business will be built on a strong foundation.

You now have a strong identity for your business. You know who you are, who your customers are, and how to explain your philosophy. Now when the cat asks you where you're going, you'll know exactly what to say!

Resources
You can access forms to use as a template at www.NWpersonaltraining.com.

CHAPTER SEVEN
Your Marketing Toolkit

"Live your life each day as you would climb a mountain. An occasional glance toward the summit keeps the goal in mind, but many beautiful scenes are to be observed from each new vantage point."

Harold V. Melchert

How many personal training businesses have the marketing and advertising budget of a major retailer? None of us! This means we have to get our message out in a creative and cost-effective manner. Instead of using expensive advertising venues, such as television or glossy publications, we can get more "bang for our buck" by developing creative marketing strategies.

Most personal trainers rely on promotional flyers, brochures and business cards to market themselves—these are must-haves for all small businesses. But how many of you have taken a marketing and advertising or graphic layout course? Although we trainers focus our energies on exercise science, many of us attempt to design and lay out our own marketing materials. And guess how many make errors that are costly—moneywise and timewise!

First impressions count. People will size up your credibility within a few seconds of viewing your brochures, flyers, letterhead and business cards. I strongly encourage you to consult with a graphic artist or marketing consultant when designing all marketing materials. It will cost you money in the beginning, but in the long term, not only will it save you the expense of unforeseen errors, it will ensure the right message is getting to the right group of potential clients.

Once you've made the decision to seek expert advice, you've got to determine who is the expert in your area. Look in the yellow pages. Ask friends, clients or family members for referrals. My husband and I interviewed 4 different businesses when we started NorthWest Personal Training & Fitness Education. We asked to see samples of each company's work and made our decision based on what we saw.

A graphic artist developed our logo, brochure, stationery and business cards. It cost us U.S.$1,500, but the result is an image that we are pleased with, says what we want it to say, and can be used on an ongoing basis. Take all your ideas and the tips I've given you and have an expert fine-tune them to create the ideal package for you and your business. Don't settle for anything less than perfect!

Design Issues

Work with the consultant you have chosen to establish the image that accurately represents you, your particular clients and your services. (This is one place your mission statement and values come into play.) Ask her to design a logo that will represent your business and its message. As part of that image, the consultant will help ensure that the type font, colors, text and layout you use look professional and are high quality.

Nothing will shoot down your credibility more than low-quality materials. People will associate low-quality materials with a low-quality business and trainer. So invest in high-quality paper stocks and photos, and get assistance to ensure there are no glaring spelling or grammatical errors.

And, of course, be sure your message is clear. Where can people contact you? I remember looking at a beautiful brochure that had been mailed out to thousands of homes in the area. But when I searched for the address and phone number of the business, they weren't there! I was shocked to discover that the business, in its focus on ensuring a high-quality brochure, had neglected to list this pertinent information. Be sure your name, location and contact information are mentioned frequently and boldly.

Before you go to print, consider your options:

- Two colors can save you money over 4 colors, and still look professional.

- Shop at 3 printers before choosing one. Get recommendations from friends and colleagues.

- A graphic artist often has relationships with printers who will offer you a better deal than you would get if you worked with a printer on your own.

- If you're happy with your materials, purchase more stock up front—the cost is much lower.

- Be sure the colors you use project the right image. Don't choose a color just because it's your personal favorite. Certain colors evoke particular emotions, and you want to be sure that the colors you choose complement your message—one more way an expert can help.

Get Your Money's Worth!

Once you have a logo and an image you are pleased with, incorporate them into all your materials. A consistent design image of colors, logo and headline text helps people become familiar with who you are and associate you with your advertising and marketing efforts. If you remain consistent to your image year after year, people will start to instantly recognize who you are and what you do upon seeing any of your materials.

Because so many personal trainers tackle the design of their own materials, they are dissatisfied with the results and wind up reinventing their materials every year. This can become very costly, and can result in clients having to reassociate you with your advertising and marketing efforts every year. You'll never gain brand awareness for your business this way.

Be creative—and save money—by making sure your promotional pieces are designed with more than one use in mind. For example, a good letterhead can be used for price sheets, client correspondence, information packages, flyers, promotional offers or presentation packages. A brochure should be suitable for mass-mailing, posting in clubs, distributing in local businesses or mailing to a list of top prospects.

Be sure all your material is cohesive. The colors you use in your brochures should match the colors in your letterhead. And if you use a motivational quote that you really connect with on your business card, use the same one on your letterhead. Be sure the image and message you want to portray are clear in all your materials.

Must-Haves for Marketing

All personal training businesses—small or large, in-club or in-studio, outdoor or in-home—should invest in these items.

Trainer Dossier

Imagine applying for a job without submitting a résumé. It just wouldn't happen. Well, meeting a client for the first time is like going to a first interview. A good résumé or dossier will make the difference. Your dossier functions as a summary of you and your business skills. It should include your personal mission statement and vision, code of ethics, values, philosophy, educational background, experience, athletic background and credentials.

Many trainers choose to include an 8 ½ × 11 professional head shot in their dossier so potential clients can associate a name with a face. If you choose to use head shots, also include an action shot of you participating in an athletic event or fitness activity that you are very passionate about, for example, running, hiking, cycling, kayaking or completing a triathlon. Your personal dossier can be posted in your club or studio, sent to potential clients, posted in local businesses and given to all new clients.

The personal dossier is "you" focused. This is where you sell yourself and demonstrate how you are different from other personal trainers. But remember, this is not the first step to selling a client. Focus on the client first and he will be sold on you before you even bring out your personal dossier!

Putting together a personal dossier is inexpensive. The principal cost is a professional head shot, which generally costs about U.S.$50 for the photo shoot and a few copies.

I am including a sample personal dossier from NorthWest Personal Training on the next page. You can use this as a template. If you're in a club setting you can highlight several trainers on one sheet with a photo and a few bullet points for each one.

Looking Good
& Feeling Great!

Alex McMillan
PERSONAL TRAINER

PHILOSOPHY

We all know there are things we need to take care of in our lives, and somehow in the shuffle of it all, we forget about somebody very important - Ourselves. I'm not talking about putting yourself before your family and friends - "Indeed we should all prefer one another over ourselves" - but I do believe you simply need to find the time to take care of yourself. We *can* make time for health and fitness. The truth is, if we don't make time now, we may find ourselves suffering from a health concern, not having much time for anything and wishing we would have spent the few hours a week in the gym. Our ability to contribute and perform in our lives and realize our dreams is directly affected by our fitness level and our willingness to take action. Be a doer. If you are ready to make a change, want to do it in the most effective way possible, and desire lasting results, consult with a professionally certified personal trainer. You will gain more time than you spend.

CLIENT BASE

Alex's strengths include *Training that is customized for the individual, *Body shaping and toning (Timely and effective Fat Loss), *Overcoming fitness plateaus (Never get stuck again), *Limited time workouts (Effective and efficient cardiovascular & muscle conditioning), *Realistic Nutrition (Finding foods you will enjoy eating to compliment the look and lifestyle you desire), *Sport specific (Improve your competitive or recreational abilities), and keeping people fit for life.

EXPERIENCE AND CREDENTIALS

- Owner and Co-Founder of McMillan Active Group NorthWest Personal Training and Fitness Education
- National Academy of Sports Medicine Certified Personal Trainer
- APEX Certified Nutrition Fitness Professional
- IDEA Member - International Fitness Professionals Organization
- Attendance at various International Fitness conferences including:
  - IDEA International Personal Training Summit, Baltimore, MA
  - IDEA World Fitness Conference, Las Vegas, NV
  - NASM Conferences/Workshops, Vancouver, WA & Portland, OR
  - APEX Conferences/Workshops, Vancouver, WA & Portland, OR
  - CanFitPro Fitness Conference, Vancouver, BC.
  - Pharmanex Workshop (Medicinal Effects of Supplementation), Portland, OR
  - Fitness Management and Ownership Workshop, Seattle, WA

PERSONAL INTERESTS

- HIKING • RUNNING • SKIING • SNOW BOARDING • ROCK CLIMBING
- RACQUETBALL • READING • RECREATIONAL SPORTS
- PLAYING GUITAR • DOING ALL THESE THINGS WITH MY WIFE SHERRI

Northwest
PERSONAL TRAINING
& Fitness Education

Brochure/Flyer

You can create a brochure and flyer in a variety of styles. You could use an 8 ½ × 11 sheet folded in 3, or a legal-size sheet folded in 4. These sizes work nicely because they fit easily into envelopes and brochure holders. Other businesses choose postcard- or irregular-size flyers that look unique and eye-catching. Remember to get the help of a graphic artist to ensure you portray the correct image and message.

Develop brochures that are classic in style so you are not forced to re-create them every year. For example, if you include prices in your brochures, each time you increase your personal training fees, you will be forced to reprint your brochures. Create a brochure that is more "image" based, and supplement this brochure with other materials, like price sheets.

The following pages have some samples to refer to as you develop your brochure.

If you don't have a huge budget to design and print a brochure, consider the format used by On The Edge Fitness Consulting and Donna Hutchinson. The style is very clean and effective, and the brochure highlights many of the areas we've discussed, including testimonials, power words, client focus and the benefits of training.

If you're looking to promote a specialty program, see how the flyer for Colin Westerman's "First Tee—Golf and Fitness Program" gives all the information clients need to make an educated decision.

If you are in a club setting and you'd like to highlight more than just your personal training program, check out The Fitness Group's brochure. It is beautifully designed. It uses attractive photos, and the highlighted text evokes emotions and makes a call to action. The Fitness Group also uses various stand-alone cards that can be very effective and less costly than the more extensive brochure style.

The GoodLife Fitness Club uses small, postcard-size materials to attract members to its personal training services. This can be a cost-effective way to get your message out to all your members.

When doing your budgeting, consider that we printed 2,500 brochures (die cut, 2-color) for U.S.$1,670.

Stand-alone cards are less costly than a full brochure, and can be very effective.

Small, postcard-style materials can be easily mailed.

All the information clients need about the program is supplied in this flyer.

This Gift Certificate Entitles

Compliments of
THE FITNESS GROUP

To redeem you Complimentary One-on-One Personal Training Session* bring this voucher into The Fitness Group on or before February 29, 2000.

Call 634-4725 ext. 2313 for more information.

*Offer valid for those individuals who have never before been involved with The Fitness Group Personal Training Program. One voucher per person.   No cash value.

Please accept this invitation for you and a friend to try us...

$29 Starter *MEMBERSHIP*
plus a *FREE* **Starter Kit**

Your Starter Kit Includes
• An orientation session with a Personal Trainer
• A 100% cotton T-shirt
• A tanning session, or cycling class
• 2 Guest Passes to share with a friend
A $129 VALUE FOR ONLY $29!

GoodLife

OVER 40 LOCATIONS!
Call 1-800-597-1FIT for location nearest you

How your golf game can be improved
From the address position to the follow through, the golf swing is a combination of flexibi... ...gth of the backswing), strength (the ...ation (the release of the hands) and ...h). Every one of these components ...he First Tee Fitness program, leading ...ing. Combine this with increased ...robic exercise program, and you

First Tee
Golf & Fitness Program

Improve Your Fitness and Lower Your Score
with Colin Westerman

Golf and fitness have become synonymous. You need look no further than David Duval and Tiger Woods to see how they are using fitness to improve their game. A solid golf swing starts with the swinger, and the First Tee Fitness Program is designed to get you into shape for the up-coming season. It will give you the benefits of a regular exercise program (fat loss, strong immune system, increased overall strength) as well as help you develop your golfing muscles, prevent injuries and lower your scores.

...been addicted to golf for ...s a BCRPA Personal Trainer, ...and currently operates a ...olin writes a nutrition ...he fitness and nutrition ...g show.

...vide lasting benefits and ...ay's new drivers. ...ration is recommended.

Format of the program
• Work in a group with your personal trainer.
• Meet for an hour and a half each week to learn and perform strength, balance, flexibility, and coordination exercises
• One hour of personal program design is included to help determine starting weights and teach proper form
• One session takes place with a certified CPGA professional to help you improve your fundamentals

Class times
Wednesdays - 6:30 - 8:00 pm
or Thursdays - 6:30 - 8:00 pm

Location & Registration
Please call First Tee at 839-5383 for location nearest you or to register.

Cost
$325 + GST
Eight week Program - Includes:
• 10.5 hours of golf specific group training
• one hour personal training
• 1 hour CPGA golf lesson
• First Tee Fitness golf shirt

Several programs can be
highlighted in one brochure.

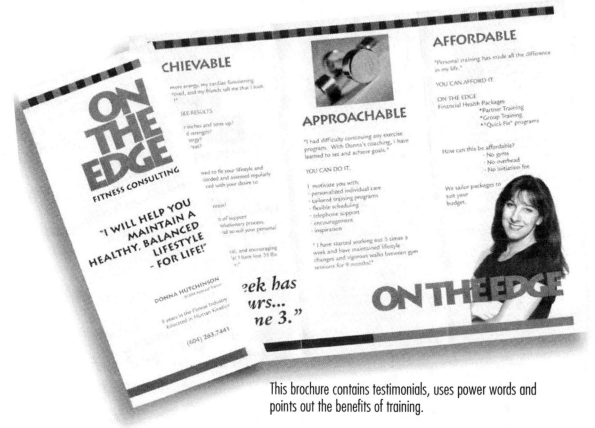

This brochure contains testimonials, uses power words and
points out the benefits of training.

Business Cards

You definitely need to invest in business cards. But they are a good investment only if you give them out regularly. After being a manager of 16 personal trainers, I know firsthand that business cards are generally purchased and then sit on shelves collecting dust.

To solve the problem, the trainers brainstormed ways to encourage regular, effective use of their business cards and came up with some helpful ideas. For example, although it costs a slightly higher fee, business cards can be designed so the back functions as a tool. The back can be used to record appointments ("My next opportunity to service you is . . ."), offer a complimentary first personal training session, give your mission statement or highlight a motivational quote you really connect with. Or you might print the formula for calculating heart rate training zones, body mass index or fat content in foods. Try to determine what would make you feel inclined to give out your cards in absolutely every situation.

If you choose to use photos in your promotional material, why not include your head shot on your card? And don't forget to include all your critical contact information. Our business cards cost U.S.$70 for 500 (double sided, 2-color).

Here are some sample business cards.

If you'd like to use a picture, Donna Hutchinson's card looks very professional. Notice that she hasn't used a photo that highlights her muscles. A card that has the personal trainer in a "pose-down" position says, "Hey, look at me. Aren't I beautiful?" and really doesn't say much about how you can help the client. But Donna's photo is very welcoming and nonintimidating. She also uses the back of her card to list some of her services.

I also like Colin Westerman's business cards. They are very clean and the graphics are appealing.

THE GIFT OF FITNESS

Share this card with someone you care about and Northwest Personal Training will offer him or her a complimentary 1st Session with us. You just might be the one directly responsible for adding years to their life and life to their years!

805 Broadway, Vancouver WA 98660
f. 360.574.7283 • e. alex@NWPersonalTraining.com
www.NWPersonalTraining.com

Looking Good & Feeling Great!

Northwest
PERSONAL TRAINING
& Fitness Education
located at PRINCETON Vancouver's Athletic Club
office: 360.574.7292
club: 360.696.0231

Alex McMillan, President
NASM & APEX Certified Personal Trainer

fitness by Colin Westerman
Nutritionist, BCRPA Personal Trainer, BSc. (food science)
phone: 604 839 5383   www.citadelhealth.com/colin

fitness by Colin Westerman
nist, BCRPA Personal Trainer, BSc. (food science)
04 839 5383   www.citadelhealth.com/colin

ON THE EDGE
FITNESS CONSULTING

DONNA HUTCHINSON
BCRPA Personal Trainer

(604) 263.7441

#301-2170 West 44th Ave.
Vancouver BC V6M 1G3
EMAIL: edgefit@home.com

"A HEALTHY BODY IS A GUEST CHAMBER FOR THE SOUL."
FRANCIS BACON

· Personal Training
· Fitness Goal Setting
· Presenter
· Nutritional Counseling
· Consulting

Letterhead/Envelopes

Letterhead functions in a variety of ways. Of course, you will use it for correspondence with new clients, potential clients or health professionals. You can also use it to print package fees, client responsibilities, waivers, information packages or any other important text.

Be sure to include all critical contact information on your letterhead. You may have space to include your mission statement and the names of your advisory board members or a motivational quote. I am including a sample of our letterhead and envelopes for you to review.

Our stationery cost us U.S.$327 for 1,000 sheets of letterhead (2-color) and U.S.$345 for 1,000 #10 envelopes (2-color).

Clothing/Uniform

What do you want your "look" to say? Athletic, professional, corporate or medical? You could choose the track suit look, which complements our industry very well. For a more corporate look, trainers wear casual dress pants and a polo shirt. This look is perhaps not as functional as a track suit but very impactful and unique. I've also seen trainers who work closely with medical professionals wear a lab-coat-style uniform. Whichever look you choose, clearly identify yourself as a personal trainer. Screen "Personal Trainer" or "Personal Fitness Trainer" or "Exercise Therapist" in big, bold letters on the back of your clothing. If someone likes what she sees when you're training a client, she will know exactly what you're doing and what to ask for when inquiring.

Approach a local sporting goods store to develop a relationship when purchasing your uniforms. I've never had to pay retail for staff uniforms. You can often get clothing at cost or even below cost if you agree to screen the sporting goods store's logo or name on your uniforms.

Web Site

Most trainers who use a Web site to market their business comment that it is most successful as a positioning tool. When you tell a prospective client that he can review more information about your business on your Web site, it instantly demonstrates that you are a professional and have a solid business.

A few years ago, Web sites were tools businesses used to explain who they were and what they did. Today, Web sites are functional entities that are used as a servicing tool. For example, on our Web site (www.NWPersonalTraining.com), clients can download client forms and start the training process before they actually see us. They can purchase their sessions online. They can review a number of educational articles and fitness programs free of charge. They can register for upcoming specialty programs or events. They can e-mail their trainer.

On the Web site of Innovative Fitness (www.InnovativeFitness.ca), clients can schedule their appointments online. Other businesses use their Web sites to post client progress information, which clients can access with a private code. The options are endless. By the time this book goes to print I imagine there will be numerous other tasks a Web site will be able to accomplish.

You can create your own Web site just as you can create your own marketing brochure, but I advise against it unless you have specialized training in this area. A poorly designed Web site can downgrade your credibility as much as a poor-quality brochure. There are a number of businesses that specialize in site design, so shop around and view their work before you make a decision.

It cost U.S.$1,500 to have someone create our Web site.

In the next chapter you'll learn about a host of promotions. They will require complementing these basic tools in your toolkit with other tools, like gift certificates. The complementary tools will be easier to compose once your image is well defined in the basic components.

CHAPTER EIGHT

Internal Marketing Promotions

"Perseverance is a great element of success. If you only knock long enough and loud enough at the gate, you are sure to wake up somebody."

Henry W. Longfellow

Promoting your services doesn't end when you gain a new client. You have to keep that client! And you have to keep looking for new customers because personal training is characterized by client turnover. **Internal promotions** may be directed to your current clients or to potential clients within your current business location.

Internal Promotions for Any Situation

All personal trainers can use the following methods to gain exposure, whether their business is in a studio, a club or clients' homes.

Complimentary First Session

Complimentary personal training sessions are necessary when you first establish your business and need to grow your client base. But any business, established or not, will benefit from offering complimentary sessions. When I first started personal training, I offered free sessions to get my name out. I was confident that once I was able to work with a potential client for just one session, I would give such great service that he would purchase a number of additional sessions. And it worked. At one point, I could guarantee I would sell the person at least one more session, but often my track record was selling 10 to 15 additional sessions. The time it took me to do the one free session was definitely worth the investment.

The Cooper Fitness Institute in Dallas, Texas, reports that its $1.5 million personal training business is a direct result of offering 3 complimentary personal training sessions to all new members. Brad Wilkins, assistant personal training director, reports that over 50% of all new members going through this system retain their personal trainer. You'll learn how to facilitate these complimentary personal training sessions in greater detail in chapter 12.

Personal Training Events (Quarterly/Monthly/Biweekly)

Offering a hiking club, a running clinic, a skiboarding and skiing trip, an indoor rock-climbing day or a kayaking trip is a great way to provide a value-added service and create wonderful friendships among your clients. They will enjoy the special treatment and be motivated to continue working with you long term.

To use these events to increase your client base, allow clients to invite their friends, colleagues or family members. It's a great way to develop a relationship with potential clients. Look for more details in chapter 5.

Health Lectures

Educational lectures and workshops are another value-added service. They empower clients to take actions to achieve their goals. Of course, you can use these lectures to gain exposure for your business by allowing clients to invite their friends, colleagues and family members.

Popular, sell-out topics include fat loss, nutrition, abdominal conditioning, back care and training for baby boomers. Try having lectures quarterly, monthly or biweekly. More information is in chapter 5.

Client Newsletter

A good client newsletter can help you establish a "community" or "family" feeling. It is a value-added service for your present clients plus a promotional tool you can distribute in clubs and local businesses and to your clients' families, friends and coworkers.

The only rule for a newsletter is to make it client focused. Profile clients and their success stories, offer fitness tips or educational articles on topics of interest to your clients or include an exercise or technique tip of the month. On a smaller, more subtle level, highlight upcoming programs or packages you are offering.

A client newsletter does not have to involve a huge time commitment. A one-page, double-sided newsletter can very easily be developed in about 2 hours with the right software. (I use Microsoft Publisher 2000 [U.S.$99.95].) After you get the hang of it, you may want to create a more extensive newsletter (4-8 pages). You don't have to do it every month. Try every 4 months, then every 3, then bimonthly. Offering the newsletter through e-mail will save the cost of printing and mailing it.

FEEDBACK FORM

We are professionals at NorthWest Personal Training and that's why it's important to us that you're getting the RESULTS you want. Please provide us with feedback so we can better service you and satisfy your needs.

Please answer the following questions and fax this form to (360) 574-7283 or return it to the reception desk attention "Alex and Sherri McMillan".

Date: _____

Name: _____ Email address: _____

Phone number: _____

1) Who is your Personal Trainer? _____

2) Do you enjoy your training sessions?   Yes   No

3) What positive feedback can you provide concerning your trainer?
_____
_____
_____
_____

4) Is there anything that your trainer could be doing differently to service you better?
_____
_____
_____

5) How has Personal Training benefited you?
_____
_____
_____
_____

6) At NorthWest Personal Training we rely on "Word of Mouth" referrals. We believe that if we service our clients so well, they'll brag about us to everyone they know. So we're not shy about asking for referrals - we really do want to help your friends, family members and co-workers. Do you know anyone who could benefit from Personal Training and would appreciate information about our services?

          Yes   No   PHONE NUMBER

NAME
1. _____   _____
2. _____   _____
3. _____

11) May we use your comments in our marketing brochures/magazines? Yes   No

Thank you very much for your time and efforts!

Looking Good & Feeling Great!

FEEDBACK FORM

Northwest **PERSONAL TRAINING** & Fitness Education

← Here's where we ask for referrals.

I'm including a few samples for you to review. (See page 54.) I really like *The Sweat Rag* by City Personal Training in Australia. It has a grassroots format you can produce on your computer, and is jam-packed with great photos of trainers working with clients. I also like Donna Hutchinson's newsletter, which is full of educational information and great contests for her clients.

Client Referral System

All personal trainers agree they receive the majority of new clients through word-of-mouth referrals. But rather than waiting around for referrals from clients, develop systems to regularly encourage them to help you grow your business.

Include "Request for Client" statements on your client feedback forms or information packages. (A copy of our feedback form, which shows how we ask for client referrals, is on page 56.) Prepare stand-alone "Give the Gift of Fitness" postcards. Learn a lesson from the real estate or financial advisory industries and ask each new client for 3 referrals. Or ask existing clients if you could send a gift certificate in their names to 5 of their friends who might be interested in personal training. Each person they name receives a complimentary gift, such as a fitness evaluation or training session.

If you decide on a variety of materials to encourage clients to list potential contacts, use slightly different wording with each piece so your approach is not redundant. Here's an example of wording that may work for you:

> *"Since you are such a valued client of XYZ Personal Training, we would like to give you the opportunity to offer one complimentary session to your loved ones. You may be the inspiration for them to start moving and experiencing many of the results you've achieved! Since it's a busy time for us, we'd like you to please limit the gift to 3 of your closest friends or family members."*

Remember to send a personal thank-you note or gift to every person who refers a new client to you. State the results the new client has achieved since starting with you, and acknowledge that the referring person was the catalyst for helping the new client take action toward her fitness goals.

Rounding Up Referrals

Personal trainers can be uncomfortable about asking for referrals. But don't be shy. Your clients train with you because they like you. And they want to see you succeed. Asking for referrals is not overstepping your boundaries. You are providing an exceptional service most people would want to share with their friends, family members and colleagues.

Here's a system to help you comfortably ask for referrals.

1. **Inform your clients of your present situation.**

   "John, I've just had a time slot open up on Tuesdays and Thursdays. Do you know anyone who might be interested in getting some help with his exercise program?"

   or

   "Sue, I've just started accepting new clients. Do you know anyone I could call to offer a complimentary initial session?"

2. **Listen for an opening.** Many of your clients will mention people in their lives who are struggling with their health and fitness. For example:

   Client: *"My husband's back has been killing him."*

   Trainer: *"Really, well why don't I call to offer him a complimentary session? I could show him some exercises to strengthen his back and abdominals."*

3. **Ask for the referral.** Get the potential client's name and number. Explain the process to your client and ask her what she would feel most comfortable with. The conversation might go like this:

   Trainer: *"This is great. John will be so pleased you thought of him. Here's what I'm going to do. I'm going to call John and let him know you've arranged a complimentary personal training session for him, and book him for an appointment. Are you comfortable with that?"*

   Client: *"That sounds great. But let me tell him first."*

   Trainer: *"Good idea. I'll make a note in my day planner to ask you about it at our next session, and then I'll contact John once you've informed him to expect my call."*

   Also be prepared to simply send a package to the potential client. Some of your clients will not feel comfortable with you calling their friends and may feel a package sent in the mail is less intrusive.

4. **Show your gratitude.** Your client has just helped you grow your business, so show your appreciation. A thank-you card or call may be all that is needed. Some trainers reward clients with a free session or a gift when they refer someone who purchases, say, 10 sessions or more.

Gift Certificates

Birthdays, anniversaries, Christmas, Valentine's Day, Mother's Day, Father's Day—take advantage of the advertising done by other businesses for these commemorations by promoting gift certificates. Most clubs experience tremendous success with this system. In fact, one club reported a 90% renewal rate from clients who started because of gift certificates. Those are very good odds! Here's a copy of the gift certificates we use. Printing cost us U.S.$160 for 500 certificates (2-color).

Internal Promotions for Fitness Facilities

If you operate your personal training business within a large health club, hospital or corporate setting, you may have 2,000+ members you can directly market to. Before you spend a great deal of time on external marketing, first saturate your internal market. Current customers are often much easier to sell. Marketing gurus suggest that people need to see a message 7 times before something actually clicks and encourages them to inquire about the product or service. Displaying your message often and professionally throughout the facility will help drive your business.

Bulletin Boards
Bulletin boards posted in highly visible places throughout a fitness area are an effective, economical way to gain exposure for your business. Use a number of bulletin boards to highlight client success stories and testimonials, benefits that people can expect to achieve when consulting with a trainer, fitness education tips from the personal training department, and upcoming personal training events/programs/lectures. One board can feature trainers' personal dossiers.

Program Flyers and Brochures
Attach brochures and flyers to all cardio machines and display them at the front desk and in washrooms, washroom stalls, the weight training room and the fitness class studio.

Club's Membership Mailing List
An easy, effective way of highlighting your services is to send a brochure or promotional flyer to all facility members. Better yet, piggyback your materials with a mailing the club is already doing. If you have access to members' e-mail addresses, you can easily and cost-effectively send regular educational tips and promotional messages to members.

Club Newsletter
Be sure to request a page or 2 within the club's newsletter to promote your services. Use a shortened version of the same information you include in your client newsletter.

Spotting in Fitness Classes
I know from experience that personal trainers who are also good, solid group fitness instructors have a very easy time growing their personal training businesses. It makes sense. If you're teaching a class to 20, 30, 50 or more, you are in the spotlight. Participants who regularly attend your classes and are thinking about consulting with a trainer are going to come to you because they already know and like you.

But not all people are cut out to be group fitness instructors, and some have no desire to put together a workout to music. So what's the next best thing? Well, if you can't be the instructor, can you be the instructor's assistant? Approach one of your club's most popular fitness instructors and suggest that you could monitor participants' technique during the muscle-conditioning segment of her fitness class. Ask if, in return, she will comment to participants on your skills and services as a trainer and the benefits people could expect to achieve from working with you. Most fitness instructors would love to have a personal assistant during their classes because it really is impossible to effectively monitor an entire class all by yourself.

Spotting/Handing Out Literature

Allocate time during the week to mingle with exercisers in the weight room and other areas of the fitness club. Talk to members, inquire about their programs and perhaps distribute fitness education material. Approach a member and let him know you have 15 free minutes between clients you could use to show him some new abdominal exercises you just learned at a conference. Or tell him you'd love to teach him how to ensure he's training in the right zone during cardio workouts.

Initiating conversation and developing a personal relationship with members will go a long way toward helping you grow your business. I've found from personal experience that when I approach a member and inquire about her program, she will frequently respond, "You know, I've been thinking about getting a trainer for a while!" Many people are just waiting for someone to approach them and initiate the process.

Developing Strong Relationships With Staff

Selling your services is so much easier if you have a lot of help. Nurture friendships among the front desk staff, group fitness instructors, other personal trainers, managers and physiotherapists. Anyone who comes in direct contact with members is in a position to promote your services. Be sure all staff members know you are accepting clients and understand how you can help members. Most important, go out of your way to help all other club staff in any way you can. Remember, if they like you, they will send you clients. And don't forget to thank them for all referrals.

Offering Special Group Personal Training

To gain exposure for the personal training program, offer specialty group training programs. These programs allow you to market your services to a lot of people at one time. Ways to facilitate group personal training programs are discussed in chapter 5.

CHAPTER NINE
External Promotions: Form Strategic Alliances

"A lot of successful people are risk-takers. Unless you are willing to do that, to have a go, to fail miserably and have another go, success won't happen."

Philip Adams

If you operate your personal training business independent of a club or larger business, you do not have a customer base to rely on for potential clients. Even if you do operate within a club setting, it is not healthy for your business to rely solely on the present club members to grow your client base. Eventually the growth of your business will plateau as you start to saturate your fitness club membership base or rely too heavily on your clients for referrals. You will have to step out of your comfort zone and start to rely on other avenues for continued business.

External promotions reach outside your current client list or work location. Relationships with local businesses, health professionals and the media will be critical for reaching your business potential.

Cross-Promotions With Other Businesses

Developing relationships with local businesses is a cost-effective way to reach a much larger market and gain greater exposure for your services. Ask yourself the following questions when determining which businesses to align with:

- What type of client do I want to attract to my personal training business?
- Where does this type of client shop or spend his time and money?
- Are any of the businesses this client patronizes in a 10- to 15-minute driving radius from me?

- Do I have any close contacts with any of these businesses? (It's always easiest to approach someone who knows and likes you!)
- Which 3 businesses could I go to tomorrow to initiate a cross-promotion?

Here's how you might approach a local retail business owner:

Trainer: *"Hey Phil, I have a great idea I think you'll really like!"*

Phil: *"Oh yeah?"*

Trainer: *"Here's how it works. I put together this gift certificate [show sample] you can hand out to all your customers. We set it up so that, for example, for every purchase of $100 or more, your customers will receive a complimentary personal training session from me courtesy of you. I put your name and logo right on top of the certificate. This program will offer more value and savings to your customers. It'll be a special way to thank your customers for shopping at your store. What do you think?"*

Phil: *"I think it's a great idea, but what will it cost me?"*

Trainer: *"Would you do it if it were free?"*

Phil: *"Yeah, of course!"*

Trainer: *"Then it's settled. I'll take care of all the details. All you have to do is distribute the gift certificate to your customers when they purchase something from you."*

Can you imagine businesses not wanting to offer something extra to their loyal customers? They have nothing to lose. And instantly you have an entire business promoting your services and helping you develop your client base. Here are guidelines to help you initiate this type of cross-promotion.

- Decide on the exact details of the promotion. What will the client have to purchase in order to receive the gift certificate?
- Get the weekly customer count so you know how many certificates/flyers to produce.
- Get the business's logo to put on the certificates.
- Ask for the number of employees and give them a small freebie at the end of the promotion to thank them for their support. A cross-promotion is limited by whether the staff at the business supports it. Get staff members on your side from the beginning by letting them know they will get something in return for their enthusiasm. The most obvious incentive is one or 2 complimentary personal training sessions for each employee.
- Run this promotion a maximum of 2 weeks. If you drag the promotion on, it can get monotonous and the staff may start to lose enthusiasm.

- Specify to the business that the certificates must be treated like money. They are not to be left in the open where anyone can pick them up. Careless treatment would devalue the offer. Certificates should be offered at the point of sale when the cashier is returning change and giving a receipt.

- Encourage the business to advertise the promotion in display windows, throughout the store and in any media advertising. Making customers aware of the promotion may encourage them to purchase more goods.

- Provide your marketing materials to help the business advertise the promotion. Include your head shot, brochures and personal dossier.

It is acceptable to do promotions with different businesses at different times. For example, each month focus on a new local business. Your name will get around quickly, and other businesses will start asking you to work with them also.

The following are good businesses to align with and potential customer approaches:

Sporting Goods Stores

"Purchase a treadmill/set of hand weights/multipurpose resistance machine and receive a complimentary personal training session. A trainer will come to your home and show you how to safely and effectively use the equipment."

Spas

"Purchase a facial/massage/body wrap and receive a complimentary personal training session for the complete mind-body-spirit package."

Flower Shops

"Purchase a bouquet of flowers for your mom, and she receives a complimentary personal training session. Help keep Mom healthy forever!"

Gardening Shops

"Do you notice your knees ache after a day of gardening? Purchase $100 worth of gardening supplies and we'll send you a personal trainer who will design a program to strengthen your body so it can handle the demands of hours of gardening."

Candy Stores

"Worried about your special someone getting fat from all the chocolate? Don't worry! Buy the chocolate for your honey and we'll throw in a complimentary personal training session to ensure he takes the pounds off as quickly as he put them on!"

Golf Centers

"Does your back ache after 18 holes? Purchase $100 worth of golfing equipment and we'll throw in a complimentary personal training session."

Adventure Travel Agencies

"Book a hiking trip to the Grand Canyon and we'll provide a complimentary personal training session to make sure your body is ready for the adventure."

Added Benefits

Developing relationships with local businesses may open up many opportunities. For example, businesses may allow you to:

- Permanently post and distribute your promotional flyers and brochures for customers.
- Use their space to host educational lectures for customers.
- Purchase their customer list so you can mail promotional flyers or brochures.
- Piggyback your brochures with one of their mailings in return for complimentary sessions.

Initiating strong relationships within your community can only benefit your business. Start with one cross-promotion, measure the success and then continue with other promotions.

Strategic Alliances With Professionals

Health or business professionals who support you and your services can help you generate more business and build a professional and credible image. Here are some ideas to help you initiate a relationship with various professionals in your community.

- Establish an 8- to 12-member advisory board that includes a massage therapist, a physiotherapist, a nutritionist, a sports physician and a chiropractor, as well as other appropriate health professionals. Complete your advisory board with a marketing and advertising specialist, a banker, an accountant, a lawyer and a successful business owner. These professionals can provide suggestions for improving your marketing initiatives and other aspects of your business. Meeting once or twice a year and being available to answer your questions are their only commitments as board members.

In return for their time and energy, offer board members VIP rates on personal training. Provide them with exposure by listing their names on your letterhead and brochures and posting their pictures and bios within your club, studio or office. Their involvement makes them instant salespeople for your business. You are never too small a business to have an advisory board.

Looking Good & Feeling Great!

PHYSICIAN APPROVAL FOR PHYSICAL ACTIVITY

Client/Patient: _____

Personal Trainer: _____ Date: _____

Date: _____

Your patient desires to engage voluntarily in the NorthWest Personal Training and Fitness Education Program. The primary objective of our program is the promotion of holistic health and fitness through personally prescribed physical activity. A certified Personal Trainer will design the individualized exercise program.

The program includes periodic physical fitness assessments and supervised exercise. The supervised exercise programs include aerobic, muscle and flexibility conditioning. All programs follow the guidelines established by the American College of Sports Medicine, unless otherwise specified. All Personal Trainers are certified in CPR, Fitness First Aid and hold national certifications.

_____ is under my care and there participation in an exercise program.

_____ is under my care and there ipation in an exercise program (describe below).

_____

_____

_____ is under my care and due e in an exercise program.

_____ M.D. Date: _____

Thank you for your assistance!

Northwest PERSONAL TRAINING & Fitness Education

Northwest PERSONAL TRAINING & Fitness Education

Looking Good & Feeling Great!

March 17, 2000

New Client's Doctor
11707 NW 34th Ave.
Vancouver, WA
98685

Advisory Board Members

DR. WAYNE LATIMER, D.C.
Chiropractic Care and
Sports Medicine

SHARON FROBERG
LMT, LMP, NCTMB
Massage Therapist

TINA SAKER, P.T.
Physical Therapist

MIKE & DARLENE PARNELL, B.A.
Marketing

LARRY E. KJELDEN, EA, ABA
Accounting

JEROME F. ELINE, J.D.
Legal

RUSS OYER, B.S.
Community Relations

Dear New Client's Doctor,

New client has recently enrolled in our Personal Training program. We realize that the relationship between an individual's physician and personal trainer is critical to obtaining their fitness program, please forward, in comments or suggestions for their fitness program, please forward, in confidence, this information for us to implement immediately.

Our NorthWest Personal Trainers provide motivation, inspiration, safety and education to our clients. Quality and safety of training is our primary concern. By developing a network of professional physicians like yourself, who support exercise and good nutrition and provide us with expert advice, we can ensure we continue to provide exceptional services to our clients.

We have included some information about our company, and it's mission, vision and values. If you have any questions or concerns, please feel free to contact us at 360.574.7292.

Thank you for your time.

Yours in health and fitness,

Alex and Sherri McMillan

Rob Cloke
NASM Personal Trainer

Ps. We've enclosed a Physician Approval for Physical Activity form. Can you please complete the form and fax it to us at 360.574.7283.

Training Center located at PRINCETON Vancouver's Athletic Club • 805 Broadway, Vancouver WA 98660
office: 360.574.7292 • club: 360.696.0231 • f. 360.574.7283 • e. info@NWPersonalTraining.com • www.NWPersonalTraining.com

- Ask all new clients to fill out a medical questionnaire, list their health professionals and sign a form giving you permission to contact these professionals. Send each client's physician or health professional a letter explaining that his or her patient has initiated an exercise program with you. Introduce your services and credentials and include your brochure, personal dossier and 5 complimentary personal training sessions for the health professional to offer to other patients who would benefit from a fitness/ wellness program. I am including a copy of the letter we send to physicians.

Alliances With Residential Complexes

Many apartment complexes and condominiums (a "condo" is an apartment that is independently owned) are equipped with a small workout studio that is the perfect size for a personal training business. These studios are often unused because the residents aren't familiar with the equipment and don't know how to use it safely and effectively. By offering personal training at condos, you help develop a fun, community atmosphere, ensure the safety of exercisers and put the space to use.

Establishing a business in a complex requires a plan. First, identify a good neighborhood. (Statistics on personal training suggest a middle- to high-income area is best.) Look for existing or soon-to-be-built complexes that provide a fitness facility for residents. Once you've targeted a few locations, speak to a manager. Introduce yourself and ask a few questions regarding the complex and the fitness studio. For example:

Does the fitness studio get used regularly?
Most often it doesn't, so you can use this as a selling point for your services.

Do you think residents would enjoy having someone show them how to use the equipment correctly?
The answer to this question is always "yes"—so you have another selling point.

Have all the condos been sold?
If they haven't, convince the decision makers they will have an easier time selling units if the complex provides a personal trainer for residents.

Is it important to have a community atmosphere among the residents of the complex?
This is always important, and you can use a number of methods to develop this atmosphere.

You can even ask for a tour of the facility. During this initial contact, it's very important to develop a friendly relationship with the manager. Instantly you'll have someone on your side. Let the manager know you'd like to propose a personal training program for the complex. Ask for the name, number and address of the decision maker. (It may be the manager, an owner or owners' association, or a strata council.)

Send a letter to the decision maker saying you've spoken to the manager (use the manager's name) and toured the fitness studio. Provide a package with information about your company, and suggest that you and the facility could work together for your mutual benefit. Promise that you'll call in a month to schedule an appointment.

A month later, call and reintroduce yourself. Ask to schedule an appointment to share the opportunities you'd like to offer the complex. You'll have a better chance of getting an appointment if you position your request by saying that you'd like to give something rather than that you *want* something.

When you meet with the decision makers, present your insurance coverage, personal dossier, promotional flyers and brochures, fees, references and proposal. Pitch the idea by demonstrating how training is a win-win-win proposition for the residents, the complex and your business. Some services you could provide to residents are:

- 2 complimentary personal training sessions each
- a health and fitness newsletter
- organized group health and fitness activities (e.g., hiking trips, walking clinics, kayaking trips)
- fitness lectures

Most often you'll be able to access the facility and a place to conduct your business free of charge. Many personal trainers have established this type of arrangement and operate their entire business with very little overhead—no rent (or a very small fee), no utilities, no equipment leasing fees, etc. It can't get any better than that.

Once the proposal is approved, distribute flyers and brochures to residents; network with the doorman and real estate agents; and host lectures, events and fitness fairs for the residents. Post fitness tips, client success stories and testimonials. Give brochures to the concierge and prominently display them at key locations in the building. Imagine how efficient you could be if all your customers lived in the same location and came to you! Don't be discouraged if you get turned down on your first try. Keep at it because nailing just one arrangement will make all your time and energy worthwhile.

Media Alliances

Who has the money to take out ads in magazines or newspapers or create a commercial for the radio or television? If you're like most fitness businesses, you don't! There is a way to get free advertising, but you do have to work for it.

- Develop a list of key media contacts for print, radio and television in your area.

- Complete regular mailings, e-mails and faxes to develop relationships. Tease media contacts with health and fitness information. For example, state, "I was just at IDEA's international health and fitness conference in Las Vegas, and I learned some of the most incredible exercises for the abdominals. It's stuff you've never seen before. Call me if you'd like to hear more about it," or "I was just at the IHRSA show in San Francisco and I've got to tell you about some of the hottest and craziest new equipment on the market."

- Offer a human interest story relating the success of one of your clients (with the client's approval of course).

- Whet the media's taste buds and you can expect at least one or 2 calls from each of your efforts. Each time your idea is used, you will be mentioned as the health and fitness expert. Ask that your business and phone number be listed so people can contact you if they have further questions.

- Offer to write a free weekly/monthly fitness column. The advertising value will be well worth the time spent writing the articles.

- Offer key media contacts a couple of complimentary sessions so they can try out your services and see what you're all about. Propose a "Media Fitness Challenge" or "Getting Into Shape Challenge" with reporters and producers of rival networks racing to improve their fitness. The press you get will be huge.

When I first moved to Vancouver, British Columbia, and developed my new business, I started faxing and mailing to media contacts. At first the response was poor. But after a few months, I started to get at least one or 2 calls for every effort. Soon I was quoted in various sources and asked to appear on local radio and television shows for 3- to 5-minute guest fitness appearances. In the beginning, I wrote many free articles and did many free appearances, but the exposure I got was priceless. Then I had my first big break. The *Province Newspaper*, our daily provincial newspaper with a very large circulation, asked me to write a weekly fitness column. And it was actually offering to pay me! Three years later, I'm still writing for this paper every Monday. Can you imagine how much it would have cost me to purchase the type of exposure I have received?

As a result of the newspaper exposure, I was asked by a local publisher to write a book. One year later *Go For Fit, The Winning Way to Fat Loss* was printed and launched. I have been asked to write by national and international magazines like *Chatelaine* and *Shape*. All this exposure resulted from committing to do some work for free in the beginning. Remember, what goes around, comes around. And your efforts will not go unnoticed!

More Promotion Opportunities

What else can you possibly do? Every little bit of exposure helps. Try some of these ideas:

- Read the newspaper. Send a congratulations card to businesspeople who have been promoted or have won an award and offer them a complimentary personal training session.

- Get involved in business organizations. For example, join the National Association of Women Business Owners, the Rotary Club, your local chamber of commerce or the Young Entrepreneurs Organization.

- Write an article for a local bank's newsletter.

- Attend a local sports medicine conference.

- Book yourself as a guest speaker at Rotary Club meetings, church group gatherings or corporate events.

- Donate your services to, or provide sponsorship for, charity events—fundraisers, auctions and races. (Commit yourself to 3-4 events like this a year.)

- Mail your brochures or flyers to homes within a 10-minute driving radius of your business. Budget to mail at least 7 times a year to about 1,000 prospects. One mailing is not enough to have impact.

- Consider how you can increase readership of your brochures. For example, everybody reads postcards, so make an offer on the back of one. Or send out your brochures stuffed in a special delivery envelope. That'll get people's attention. A direct-mail piece does you no good if no one reads it.

- Use trade directories to mail to a specific audience. For example, if you want to target the legal profession, look in the directory of the local bar association (found in most libraries or on the Internet).

- You will eventually find it necessary to take out an ad in the yellow pages and you will be surprised at how costly it can be. Start small and grow the size of your ad as your revenues warrant.

- Write advertorials in trade journals. An advertorial is an article you write and pay for as if it were advertising. An advertorial can often position you as an expert better than an advertisement can.

- Advertise in professional publications targeting lawyers, accountants, bankers, doctors. This is more cost-effective than advertising in general interest publications, since it targets the population you're trying to attract.

- Consider selling merchandise that promotes your business, such as calendars, clothing or water bottles.

- Advertise your business with a sign on your vehicle. You'll be promoting your business everywhere you go.

Finally, talk about your business with everyone you meet. Any and all situations can function as an opportunity to grow your business and develop your client base.

CHAPTER TEN
What Is Your Marketing Strategy?

"High on the wall, in the castle of your dreams of success, hangs the picture of what you want to be. Always keep that picture hanging there. Night and day dream of what you intend to be . . . . All successes are, at first, dreams."

Fred Van Amburgh

At this point, you have a solid understanding of your business and how you would like to be positioned against your competitors. You have identified your target markets, your marketing messages and the tools you'll need. You have a good understanding of a variety of internal and external marketing options. Now let's put all this information together into a plan by tackling your marketing and advertising strategy.

Marketing and Advertising Plan Pointers

- Decide which ideas function well within your value system and style, then decide how you will facilitate these ideas throughout the year. You can't feasibly host all events and promotions at all times throughout the year.

- Determine the time lines for the campaigns. Which campaigns will be ongoing, which will you offer a few times throughout the year and which will be offered only once a year?

- Examine each month for holidays, time of year (for seasonal programs), and special local events, to ensure your promotions complement what is going on in your community.

- Establish which internal and external promotions you'll conduct each month.

On the following pages you'll find our marketing plan to use as a template and a blank worksheet.

Develop Your Plan

Must-Haves

Check off each item once you're happy with the look of it:

- ❏ Personal dossier
- ❏ Brochure/flyer
- ❏ Business cards
- ❏ Price sheet
- ❏ Letterhead/envelopes
- ❏ Clothing/uniform

Internal Promotions

Internal promotions to offer within the next year:

_____

_____

_____

_____

External Promotions

External promotions to develop within the next year:

_____

_____

_____

_____

Sample Yearly Marketing Plan

JANUARY 2000

Internal Marketing:
- Bulletin boards
- "Knowledge Is Power" workshop—"Getting Started!"
- Complimentary sessions
- Blitz program—"New Year's Resolution Solution"
- Newsletter
- Fitness tip e-mails
- Promotional flyers
- Client mailings or e-mailings: New Year's greetings & updates on upcoming programs

External Advertising & Marketing:
- Cross-promotions—weight loss clinic
- Ongoing networking
- Yellow pages

Programs:
- Running clinic
- Training camp

Special Packages:
- None

Client Building:
- Skiing/boarding trip

FEBRUARY 2000

Internal Marketing:
- Bulletin boards
- "Knowledge Is Power" workshop—golf conditioning
- Complimentary personal training sessions
- Blitz program—"New Year's Resolution Solution"
- Newsletter
- Fitness tip e-mails
- Promotional flyers

External Advertising & Marketing:
- Cross-promotions—candy store
- Ongoing networking
- Yellow pages

Programs:
- "Back Care 101"

Special Packages:
- Valentine's Day gift ideas
- Partner training package deal

Client Building:
- Indoor rock climbing

MARCH 2000

Internal Marketing:
- Bulletin boards
- "Knowledge Is Power" workshop—none
- Complimentary personal training sessions
- Blitz program—"Spring Into Shape"
- Newsletter
- Fitness tip e-mails
- Promotional flyers

External Advertising & Marketing:
- Cross-promotions—adventure travel store
- Ongoing networking
- Yellow pages

Programs:
- Golf conditioning

Special Packages:
- None

Client Building:
- None

APRIL 2000

Internal Marketing:
- Bulletin boards
- "Knowledge Is Power" workshop—fat loss
- Complimentary personal training sessions
- Blitz program—"Spring Into Shape"
- Newsletter
- Fitness tip e-mails
- Promotional flyers

External Advertising & Marketing:
- Cross-promotions— gardening shop
- Ongoing networking
- Yellow pages

Programs:
- Training camp

Special Packages:
- Mother's Day special

Client Building:
- "Fit for Heart" event

MAY 2000

Internal Marketing:
- Bulletin boards
- "Knowledge Is Power" workshop —triathlon training camp
- Complimentary personal training sessions
- Blitz program—"Summer Fix"
- Newsletter
- Fitness tip e-mails
- Promotional flyers

External Advertising & Marketing:
- Cross-promotions—flower shop
- Ongoing networking
- Yellow pages

Programs:
- Running clinic
- "Abs 101"

Special Packages:
- Mother's Day special

Client Building:
- None

JUNE 2000

Internal Marketing:
- Bulletin boards
- "Knowledge Is Power" workshop —"Training Baby Boomers"
- Complimentary personal training sessions
- Blitz program—"Summer Fix"
- Newsletter
- Fitness tip e-mails
- Promotional flyers

External Advertising & Marketing:
- Cross-promotions—clothing shop
- Ongoing networking
- Yellow pages

Programs:
- Outdoor training camp
- Training camp

Special Packages:
- Father's Day special

Client Building:
- Hiking club

JULY 2000

Internal Marketing:
- Bulletin boards
- "Knowledge Is Power" workshop—none
- Complimentary personal training sessions
- Blitz program—"Summer Fix"
- Newsletter
- Fitness tip e-mails
- Promotional flyers

External Advertising & Marketing:
- Cross-promotions—restaurant
- Ongoing networking
- Yellow pages

Programs:
- None

Special Packages:
- None

Client Building:
- White-water rafting

AUGUST 2000

Internal Marketing:
- Bulletin boards
- "Knowledge Is Power" workshop—none
- Complimentary personal training sessions
- Blitz program—"Summer Fix"
- Newsletter
- Fitness tip e-mails
- Promotional flyers

External Advertising & Marketing:
- Cross-promotions—restaurant
- Ongoing networking
- Yellow pages

Programs:
- None

Special Packages:
- None

Client Building:
- Kayaking
- "Hood to Coast" relay team

SEPTEMBER 2000

Internal Marketing:
- Bulletin boards
- "Knowledge Is Power" workshop—"Using Supplements to Help Achieve Your Goals"
- Complimentary personal training sessions
- Blitz program—"Fall Into Fitness"
- Newsletter
- Fitness tip e-mails
- Promotional flyers

External Advertising & Marketing:
- Cross-promotions—clothing store
- Ongoing networking
- Yellow pages

Programs:
- Running clinic
- "Legs 101"
- Training camp

Special Packages:
- None

Client Building:
- Inline skating

OCTOBER 2000

Internal Marketing:
- Bulletin boards
- "Knowledge Is Power" workshop—"Ouch, My Aching Back!"
- Complimentary personal training sessions
- Blitz program—"Fall Into Fitness"
- Newsletter
- Fitness tip e-mails
- Promotional flyers

External Advertising & Marketing:
- Cross-promotions—baby clothing store
- Ongoing networking
- Yellow pages

Programs:
- Skiing & boarding camp

Special Packages:
- None

Client Building:
- None

NOVEMBER 2000

Internal Marketing:
- Bulletin boards
- "Knowledge Is Power" workshop—"Building Muscle"
- Complimentary personal training sessions
- Blitz program—"Holiday Blitz Buster"
- Newsletter
- Fitness tip e-mails
- Promotional flyers
- Client mailings: Christmas cards, party invites & gift certificates

External Advertising & Marketing:
- Cross-promotions—ski shop
- Ongoing networking
- Yellow pages

Programs:
- Training camp

Special Packages:
- None

Client Building:
- None

DECEMBER 2000

Internal Marketing:
- Bulletin boards
- "Knowledge Is Power" workshop—none
- Complimentary personal training sessions
- Blitz program—"Holiday Blitz Buster"
- Newsletter
- Fitness tip e-mails
- Promotional flyers

External Advertising & Marketing:
- Cross-promotions—spa
- Ongoing networking
- Yellow pages

Programs:
- None

Special Packages:
- Holiday packages

Client Building:
- Christmas party

Yearly Marketing Plan Worksheet

For each month list the promotions or campaigns you would like to offer.

JANUARY

Internal Marketing:

_____
_____
_____
_____

External Advertising
& Marketing:

_____
_____

Programs:

_____

Special Packages:

_____

Client Building:

_____

FEBRUARY

Internal Marketing:

_____
_____
_____
_____

External Advertising
& Marketing:

_____
_____

Programs:

_____

Special Packages:

_____

Client Building:

_____

MARCH

Internal Marketing:

_____
_____
_____
_____

External Advertising
& Marketing:

_____
_____

Programs:

_____

Special Packages:

_____

Client Building:

_____

APRIL

Internal Marketing:

_____
_____
_____
_____

External Advertising
& Marketing:

_____
_____

Programs:

_____

Special Packages:

_____

Client Building:

_____

MAY

Internal Marketing:

_____
_____
_____
_____

External Advertising
& Marketing:

_____
_____

Programs:

_____

Special Packages:

_____

Client Building:

_____

JUNE

Internal Marketing:

_____
_____
_____
_____

External Advertising
& Marketing:

_____
_____

Programs:

_____

Special Packages:

_____

Client Building:

_____

JULY

Internal Marketing:

_____

_____

_____

_____

External Advertising
& Marketing:

_____

_____

Programs:

_____

Special Packages:

_____

Client Building:

_____

AUGUST

Internal Marketing:

_____

_____

_____

_____

External Advertising
& Marketing:

_____

_____

Programs:

_____

Special Packages:

_____

Client Building:

_____

SEPTEMBER

Internal Marketing:

_____

_____

_____

_____

External Advertising
& Marketing:

_____

_____

Programs:

_____

Special Packages:

_____

Client Building:

_____

OCTOBER

Internal Marketing:

_____

_____

_____

_____

External Advertising
& Marketing:

_____

_____

Programs:

_____

Special Packages:

_____

Client Building:

_____

NOVEMBER

Internal Marketing:

_____

_____

_____

_____

External Advertising
& Marketing:

_____

_____

Programs:

_____

Special Packages:

_____

Client Building:

_____

DECEMBER

Internal Marketing:

_____

_____

_____

_____

External Advertising
& Marketing:

_____

_____

Programs:

_____

Special Packages:

_____

Client Building:

_____

Marketing Follow-Up

- Keep a detailed record of which promotions work and which ones don't. Be sure to ask all new clients how they heard about you. Record how many people take advantage of every promotional offer you advertise. Record the amounts of revenues generated by each promotional campaign.

- Develop your selling skills. You don't want to spend a great deal of time, energy and money encouraging people to inquire about your services and then be unable to sell them on your personal training packages. (There's sales help in the upcoming chapters.)

- Understand that you must always exceed customer expectations. Once you've sold clients on personal training sessions, you want to keep them long term. It is much easier to retain clients than to continually recruit new ones.

CHAPTER ELEVEN

Easy Selling: The First Contact

"Better a poor man who walks in his integrity than he who is crooked in his ways and rich."
Proverbs 28:6

Have you taken a sales training course? Many personal trainers are uncomfortable with selling. They'd like the client to hurry up and buy the sessions so they can get going on what they know and do best. Trainers are scared of pushing the "hard sell" or being too aggressive. Unfortunately, a solid marketing campaign will be ineffective if you're not skilled at selling your services once you've got someone in the door.

To succeed as a personal trainer, you must become a top-notch salesperson. Holding the highest credentials will make no difference if you can't get clients to purchase sessions with you. Possessing an exceptional personality and an amazing ability to motivate will not matter if you can't convince clients to invest in your services. Developing sales skills not only enables you to generate a higher income but also allows you to impact more people's lives.

Let's start off by correcting a misconception. "Closing the sale" is the term used to describe the process of asking for the client's money. The term can have a negative meaning to trainers who associate it with pressure tactics. But in my philosophy, you do not need to be a high-pressure salesperson or use unsavory tactics. If you enter communications with a potential client with "closing" as your primary goal, you will quickly lose the client. To me closing the sale is, in fact, opening or developing a relationship. That is how you sell with integrity.

A good salesperson does not focus on "selling" a person but rather on *servicing the person*. Before any interaction with a potential client, ask yourself, "How can I help this individual? What are her needs?" Once you have identified her needs, simply decide whether your services can meet those needs. If so, then tell her about your services, or offer a sample. That's it.

I know you are not a personal trainer because you love selling but because you love helping people. But you need to sell to get people to experience your services! Remember that selling is not a bad thing! You are selling very good things: improved health and fitness, more energy, enhanced confidence and self-esteem, longevity. You must believe in yourself and your services. Remember that if a person has called you or inquired about your services, she is interested. She is just waiting for you to explain how you can help.

Focus on the Client

When you identified the types of clients you wanted to serve, you also identified their needs and developed messages to explain how you could meet those needs. The focus was on the clients. Carry that philosophy through when you talk to potential clients.

Here's an example of how you could approach an individual in a club setting with the purpose of addressing her needs:

Trainer: *"Hi there. My name is Sherri and I'm a personal trainer here. Are you new to the club?"*

Prospect: *"Yes, I am."*

Trainer: *"I thought so. What's your name?"*

Prospect: *"Karen."*

Trainer: *"Well, welcome to the club, Karen. Hey, I know when you first join a new club, you sometimes have questions about the equipment or where things are or proper club etiquette. I'd love to take you through a complimentary personal training session—all new members get one. Have you always exercised, or are you just getting started? Do you have any injuries? What are your goals? Why don't I book you for some time in the next few days to get you started off on the right foot?"*

In this interaction, you enter the conversation with the assumption that this individual has some needs you can serve. Focusing on her needs makes it very easy for you to communicate. A first encounter that does not intimidate someone or make her feel pressured to buy is critical. Your role is to welcome the new member and make her feel comfortable and safe with you. You may feel even more comfortable if you limit the initial encounter to introducing yourself to the new member and getting to know her name. Then the next couple of times you see her, say "hi," use her name, and perhaps comment on her consistency. Then, maybe at the third or fourth contact, discuss how you could help her, and book her for a complimentary session. This will ensure you have developed a relationship before you try to "sell" the member on your services.

Remember, your knowledge of physiology will be wasted unless you immediately connect with your potential client and develop her trust. She will know if you are only trying to sell her or you genuinely desire to help her. Just telling a potential client what she wants to hear may sometimes help you close the sale in the short term. However, if a person perceives you have "pulled a fast one," you will quickly lose that person. Success as a personal trainer depends on your ability to *keep* your clients, not just sell them.

We all purchase things regularly, so each of us has experienced the sales process. Think of a recent sales experience you had in a department store, at a car dealership or in a hardware store. Think about a time when you were happy to buy a product or service, or bought more than you originally thought you would. What qualities did the salesperson demonstrate in that encounter? Then think about a time when you've been unhappy with a sales experience. What qualities did the salesperson demonstrate in that experience? We all know what it takes to be a good or bad salesperson; we just need to apply that knowledge to our business.

Phone Power Skills

Since much of your business is initiated on the phone, it's imperative to understand how you can use this tool to your advantage. I have been fortunate enough to receive extensive training on using the telephone to complete business. Here are a few guidelines I've learned:

- Place the phone where it is the center of attention. It is difficult to perform well on the phone when distractions and disruptions are occurring around you.

- Pay attention to your posture while talking. Sounding energetic is not easy if you're reclined in an easy chair or slouched on the couch. Try putting a long cord on the phone or use a headset or cell phone so you can move around while talking. Remember, your body language can be heard!

- Consciously attempt to add more tone, animation and energy to your voice.

- Make important calls when you're feeling most upbeat and energetic. Perhaps you'll find making calls right after a workout or first thing in the morning works for you. Get yourself psyched up.

I'm not quite sure whether answering machines make life easier or more difficult. Many personal trainers complain of "playing tag" with answering machines. Here are some suggestions to help you use answering machines to your advantage.

- The message you leave on your own answering machine may be the first contact a potential client has with you. In an upbeat, energetic and positive voice, tell callers a little about your business and how you can help clients. Perhaps finish with an inspirational quote or message.

- When leaving a message on a potential client's machine, tell the person who you are and that you'd like to talk with her in detail about her goals. Leave your phone/pager number and a specific time you can be reached. Convey excitement, enthusiasm and energy in your voice. Also, leave a time when you will call back—and be sure to call back at exactly that time.

- Trainers who have left numerous messages for a potential client often ask me, "How many times do I call back before I start to become a pest?" My advice is, keep calling until the person tells you not to. Remember, he is the one who inquired about your services, so he is interested. If he is very busy, he will appreciate your persistence.

- If you are experiencing the frustrating "Tag, you're it!" scenario, ask a "now" question. For example, if leaving a message with a secretary, spouse or room-mate, ask if there is an alternative cell phone, work or home number at which to reach the person you are calling. It is best to speak directly with that person.

Preparing for the First Phone Call

Do you remember the very first time you had to call about a personal training inquiry? If you weren't properly trained on making a first phone call, you probably felt very awkward, and stumbled over many of your words.

You can evolve from a trainer who lacks confidence and the right words to a trainer who is confident, eloquent and effective in that initial interaction. All it takes is practice. Role-play the telephone call, using your friends, family members and colleagues to develop your systems and scripts. It will take hours of your time at first, but you definitely don't want to practice on your clients! Role-playing telephone conversations is well worth the time invested.

On the first phone call, spend time developing a relationship and a connection. This will increase the chances of clients starting with you immediately and decrease the chances of their making similar calls to numerous personal trainers.

Some sales training experts suggest that you get a potential client off the phone and into the gym as quickly as possible. I disagree. You've got a potential client on the phone. This is your first opportunity to develop a relationship with her, so take advantage of it. Invest some time and energy into getting to know this person. Do you honestly think you have to be with someone in person for a relationship to develop? Not at all! How would you explain all the marriages that have occurred as a result of e-mail connections?

The worst mistake salespeople make is talking about themselves. If you [want] the potential client to like you, avoid talking about yourself and instead spe[nd the] majority of the time asking the client questions about herself. Ask guided que[stio]ns, but let her do the talking. Listen and paraphrase. Your goal is to listen to the client 60% of the time, give her information 25% of the time, and spend only 15% of the time getting her commitment.

Be sure you have a script close by to refer to, paper for notes, and your personal training promotional package and price list.

Protocol for a First Phone Call

1. **Introduction.** The introduction is the first thing you will say to the client. This will set the mood of the conversation. It should be precise and lead you into the rest of the conversation.

   "Hi, is Sandy there? Hi, Sandy, this is Sherri calling from XYZ Personal Training. I understand you're interested in personal training. Do you have a few moments to chat?"

2. **History.** During this stage, get as much information about the client as possible. Discuss her fitness background. Determine what exercise she's doing—how often, how long and how much. Get as much information as possible on all parts of her fitness program: cardio, muscle conditioning and flexibility. Discuss nutrition, injury status, sleeping habits and stress levels. Listen for key pieces of information. Is she a beginner? Is there an injury you can help rehabilitate? Is she neglecting key fitness components that you can address?

   I liken this stage to a conversation you might have at a party. If you're at a party and you want someone to like you, you ask a ton of questions. People love to talk about themselves. If you let them do so, they will leave their interactions with you thinking you are just an amazing person even though you haven't told them anything about yourself. So engage your potential client in interactive conversation. Be sure to be interested in what she's saying.

3. **Goals.** Find out exactly why the client needs you. Be sure to probe so you are very clear about her expectations.

4. **Action Plan.** Here's where you get to explain how you can help. Be sure to relate everything you say back to what the client told you. Focus on the benefits she will achieve, not the features of your program.

5. **Conclusion.** Tie up loose ends by determining how you will work together. When and how often will you train? Book the first appointment. Determine whether you will perform a basic or comprehensive fitness assessment. Tell her what she can expect during the first session. Ask her to pick up, fill out and return the client questionnaire.

Thank the client!

Here's a sample phone script:

Trainer: "Hello. Is Sue Brown there, please?"

Client: "Yes, this is Sue."

Trainer: "Hi, Sue! It's Sherri calling from XYZ Personal Training. How are you doing?"

Client: "Great!"

Trainer: "Well, Sue, I understand you're interested in personal training, so I wanted to give you a call to discuss your goals. Do you have a few minutes to chat?"

Client: "Yes, that would be great."

Trainer: "Are you currently exercising, Sue?" [If so, congratulate her. If not, tell her how great it is that she's willing to take the first step. Let her know that most people spend their entire lives just wishing they'd started exercising!]

Client: "Well, I've been exercising for about 10 years, and in the past few years I've put on a few pounds and I'm really starting to get bored with my program!"

Trainer: "It's so great that you're exercising!" [Ask as many pertinent questions as possible. Let her do the talking and you'll have yourself a client! Ask guided questions to get the information you need, e.g., "What kind of exercise are you doing? How many times per week? For how long? Do you stretch? Why do you think the exercise program isn't working anymore? Do you think your body has adapted to your program? How's your nutrition? Do you have any injuries I should know about?"]

"So, Sue, how would you like me to help you? What are your goals?"

Client: "Well, I'd like to . . . "

Trainer: [Ask guided questions so you're very clear on her goals.] "So, let me see if I've got this right. You would like to restructure your exercise program so it's more effective at burning fat; you'd like to have a leaner, more fit physique; and you'd like a program that offers more variety so you don't get bored. Is that right?"

Client: "Yeah, that's exactly it!"

Trainer: "Okay, well, I can definitely help you out! What I'll do is design a program that offers some changes so your body is forced to respond. We'll start some weight training, which you haven't been doing, and this will help raise your metabolism, making it a lot easier to burn more body fat. Weight training will also increase your muscle tone and definition. In addition, we'll set some nutrition goals to ensure that you're doing the right things. How's that sound?"

Client: "That sounds perfect."

Trainer: "Good! Now all we have to do is decide how you and I are going to work together. There are lots of options. Some of my clients train with me 4 to 5 times a week, which is an amazing method of ensuring each of your workouts is effective—but only if you can afford it. Other clients see me a couple of times a week, once a week or even just once a month.

"The most popular and economical way is to train 2 times a week with me and then do the rest of your workouts on your own. This option allows me to constantly update your program so you can advance more quickly, and commits you to coming to the gym for your more challenging workouts. What do you think would be best for you? How many times do you want to train with me in a week?"

Client: "Maybe I should try once or twice a week."

Trainer: "That's great, Sue! Why don't we start with twice a week and then you can see how it goes?"

Client: "Yeah, that would work."

Trainer: [If you want to discuss prices, you can do this now or wait until your first session. Generally, clients will ask you about prices anyway, so you might as well educate them on the options.]
"Now we should decide which personal training package you'd like to start with. We offer 50-, 35-, 20-, 15-, 10- or 5-session packages. Of course, you get a better rate with the larger packages. Since we are going to be working together 2 times per week, if you bought, for example, 20 sessions, that would allow for 10 weeks of training. You'd definitely notice significant changes by then. What do you think?"

Client: "I think I'd like to start with 10 sessions."

Trainer: "Perfect. And then at the end of 10 you can decide whether you'd like to start training on your own or renew."

Client: "Good."

Trainer: *"Sue, can you grab a pen? I'm going to give you a list of things to do before we meet for the first time. The first thing to do is get a client information package. You can stop by the reception desk at the studio to pick it up or I can e-mail or fax it to you. It is an 8-page questionnaire that outlines your health and fitness history, and details your goals and interests. This information will allow me to design the exercise program that's best for you. You can fill out the questionnaire and then return it 2 days before our first appointment. This will give me enough time to prepare for our first session. Would you like to pick the package up or would you prefer that I e-mail or fax it to you?"*

Client: *"Actually, I can pick it up on my way home from work tonight."*

Trainer: *"Okay, well, let's get started as soon as possible. When can you meet?"*

Client: *"Can you meet me on Friday at 9:00 AM?"*

Trainer: *"Yes I can! Okay, write this down. We're scheduled for Friday, July 25, at 9:00 AM. Be sure to come dressed to exercise. All you have to do is pick up the client package at the reception desk, at which time you can pay for a 10-session package. Then fill out the questionnaire in the package and return it to the reception desk, addressed to me, by Wednesday, July 23."*

Client: *"No problem."*

Trainer: *"Okay, I'll see you on Friday. I really look forward to training with you! Bye."*

Client: *"Me too! Bye."*

Make a script to help you through this initial phone consultation so you don't forget anything. But don't read from it! Use it to guide you and to make notes on.

Now you've got a clear picture of some of the things you can do before you actually book an individual for her first session with you. The next chapter will provide you with ideas on actions you can take to enhance the success of the first person-to-person contact.

CHAPTER TWELVE
Easy Selling: Conducting the First Session

"The result of any action is dependent upon the amount of confidence with which it is done."
Sathya Sai Baba

Let's imagine you're in the market for a hot new vehicle—a convertible sports car. Would you make the investment without a test-drive? No way! You've got to get a feel for the car. How's it ride? Does it handle corners well? How fast does it go from 0 to 60? Does it satisfy all your needs? Do you look good in it? These are all important questions that need to be answered before you start dishing out the cash!

Why would personal training be any different? Most people in the market for personal training are confused about what personal training is. Offering a complimentary session encourages people to test-drive your personal training services. Thoroughly impressing a potential client in the complimentary session can open up a long-term client-trainer relationship. The good news is, there are a number of options you can choose from when deciding how to offer the initial session.

First Session Options

Option 1: Complimentary First Session

It's important to note that the word "complimentary" is preferred over "free." "Free" implies a lower value than "complimentary," and although these are just words, impressions and positioning definitely count. This session begins with a consultation and finishes with movement. The advantage is that it allows a prospect to experience firsthand the service of personal training, without making a commitment.

Option 2: Complimentary First Consultation

The time in this session is spent on establishing SMART goals, developing a program outline, discussing obstacles to success and providing training recommendations. There is no movement during a consultation. The advantage is the client gets a solid program; the disadvantage is he doesn't get a chance to test-drive movement. A consultation is like going to a dealership and talking about driving a car but never getting behind the wheel.

Option 3: Complimentary Fitness Assessment

A number of businesses have found success with offering a free fitness assessment rather than a free personal training session to attract clients to their services. The assessment enables the trainer to develop a relationship with the potential client without actually providing any program design. Once the fitness assessment is completed, the trainer can point out the client's strengths and areas that need improvement and then explain how training could help him achieve his goals.

Option 4: Discounted Services

Many personal training businesses do not offer free sessions, believing that this practice devalues the service. Instead, these businesses attract clients by offering gift certificates—for example, "Bring this gift certificate to XYZ Personal Training and receive $40 off your first session," or "Call XYZ Personal Training today and receive 75% off your first session." This type of offer places value on the session because the client pays something.

Complimentary Session Pointers

I have tried all the options and they all seem to work. I do prefer providing some movement during the first session. As soon as the client begins to move, serotonin, endorphins and adrenaline are released into the bloodstream, giving the client that happy-go-lucky attitude that makes him feel better. That feeling instantly demonstrates that your services work.

It's important to establish the parameters of what you can actually accomplish during a complimentary session. For example, you may suggest:

"Rick, you've listed 4 goals here that are really important to you. I think you realize that we're not going to be able to address them all in the next half hour, so why don't we focus on what's most important to you now? What would you like to focus on in the next bit?"

Listen to the client's answer and then respond:

"Great, we can save the rest for later!"

From the very beginning, treat all "comp clients" as if they've just purchased 50 sessions. Whether or not you are conscious of it, if you believe that your comp clients will not purchase further sessions, you will treat them differently, decreasing the chances of closing the sale.

Keep a record of the outcome of complimentary sessions. For example, if you complete 4 complimentary sessions and sell 2 of the clients on 20-session packages, make note of that. Then you will know the process is definitely working in your favor. If you aren't selling additional sessions following the complimentary one, you may need to invest in more sales training or try another introductory session option. A good rule of thumb is that you can expect to sell one of 3 clients on more sessions.

The First Meeting

People come to personal trainers because they want more energy and a positive new perspective on life. They will be attracted to someone who exudes these qualities. You must demonstrate an energetic, positive, upbeat and caring personality! Let's review key concepts for your first meeting with a prospective or new client:

- Demonstrate exceptional follow-up skills right from the beginning. Call to confirm your first appointment, promptly respond to all inquiries and call clients back when you say you will. You'll impress clients with your exceptional organization and business skills.

- Project ultimate professionalism in your speech, attire and hygiene.

- Arrive early and prepared. The only way to be completely prepared is to be familiar with the client's health history, injury status, nutrition and stress concerns, present fitness level, goals and past obstacles to success. You can get some information over the phone, but you'd be surprised how much more information you get when you ask a person to write it down. I always ask potential clients to fill out an 8-page client questionnaire (see a copy on NWPersonalTraining.com), so I have detailed, documented information before the session. Clients return the questionnaire one to 2 days before their first session so I can review their answers and start to structure the program. Following this process allows me to thoroughly impress a new client by coming to the first session with a "Client Resource Package," which contains completed program design forms and educational articles relative to the client's goals.

Be prepared to fax or e-mail the questionnaire to clients who can't pick it up. I explain to all new clients that the form is lengthy but if they complete it thoroughly, I will be able to design a program that is much more personalized and effective at achieving their goals.

- The first time you meet a client, smile, introduce yourself, give a firm handshake, perhaps touch his shoulder or forearm, and be conscious of your body language (55% of the communication process, according to communication specialists) and your voice (38% of the communication process).

- If the client has never been to the gym, provide a tour. Introduce him to other staff members and clients so he feels like part of a team or family. If you're training in the client's home, take the time to meet his family so he feels comfortable with you.

- As soon as you sit down with your potential client, present the "Client Resource Package." Inside, include a few educational articles relative to his personal goals, your brochure outlining information about you and your services, copies of testimonials and your business card. Quickly review the material with him.

Do	**Don't**
• Shake hands.	• Interrupt.
• Break the ice by engaging in easy chitchat. ("Where are you from? What do you do?")	• Tap your fingers.
• Look the client in the eye.	• Get distracted by outside events.
• Lean toward the client.	• Assume you know what the client is talking about.
• Take brief notes on important points.	
• Smile to acknowledge the client.	
• Acknowledge and repeat the client's concerns.	

Option 1 or 4: Complimentary or Discounted Training Session

Total length: 1 hour

5 minutes: Greet client; tour facility; introduce client to staff and other clients.

25 minutes: Present "Client Resource Package"; set goals; review potential obstacles; discuss client and trainer responsibilities; present initial program design.

25 minutes: Introduce practical component of 4-6 new exercises or stretches, focusing on the most important of the client's goals; explain the exercises and their benefits; demonstrate; have client practice with and without resistance; quiz to ensure client understands and is able to reproduce the movements without you.

5 minutes: Review client's other goals and needs; discuss how you can help; review the options for working with you long term; suggest a package.

Option 2: Complimentary Consultation

Total length: 35 minutes to 1 hour

5 minutes: Greet client; tour facility; introduce client to staff and other clients.

25-50 minutes: Present "Client Resource Package"; conduct thorough consultation, including goal setting, review of potential obstacles, discussion of client and trainer responsibilities; present initial program design.

5 minutes: Review goals and needs; discuss how you can help; review the options for working with you long term; suggest a package.

Option 3: Complimentary Fitness Assessment

Total length: 1 hour

5 minutes: Greet client; tour facility; introduce client to staff and other clients.

40 minutes: Conduct fitness assessment, including blood pressure; resting heart rate; postural analysis; girth and skinfold measurements; submaximal cardiovascular, muscular strength and flexibility tests; and Polaroid shots. (Choose which measurements are appropriate for your organization; not all tests are required.)

10 minutes: Discuss the results of the tests; suggest program design and improvement.

5 minutes: Review goals and needs; discuss how you can help; review the options for working with you long term; suggest a package.

- If he's completed a client questionnaire, you'll be able to say things like, "I noticed that you play a bit of beach volleyball." Discuss his goals, needs and obstacles to success. Ask questions that relate to consequences and benefits:

  "How does it feel to not exercise?"

  "What will happen if you don't make changes?"

  "Why is it so important for you to make changes?"

  "What would be different if you lost 20 pounds?"

  "How would it feel if you exercised 5 times a week?"

  "How would it feel if you had a ton of energy?"

- Show the client an action plan and explain how you are going to help him. Discuss a time frame for achieving his goals.

- Use "assumptive" language, which assumes that the client will purchase more sessions and develop a long-term relationship with you. Eliminate the word "if" from your language when communicating with potential clients. For example, instead of saying, "If you decide to train with me, I'll . . .," say:

  "Once we decide how we're going to work together, I'm going to . . ."

  Or

  "For the first few months, we'll focus on technique so you do each exercise effectively and safely and then we can start to include more advanced exercises and techniques."

  This type of approach displays an exceptional level of confidence in your services.

Now you've got some ideas on how to conduct that first session with a client. But what happens when it's over? How do you convince the potential client to invest in your services? Read the next chapter.

CHAPTER THIRTEEN

Easy Selling: Overcome Your Fear of Asking

"You cannot direct which way the winds of adversity will blow, but you can adjust your sails."
Shantidasa

You've finished the session, now what? Sales gurus suggest that we fail to gain commitment to purchase on approximately 62% of prospects because we don't ask them to participate. You've got to resist your fear of asking.

Try the following questions or suggestions with prospects:

- *"What do you think would be best for you—5, 10, 15 or 20 sessions?"*
- *"Most of our clients see their trainers 2 times a week. How does that sound for you?"*
- *"We can train together a number of times each week or as little as once a month. What do you think would work for you?"*
- *"Do you want to train in the mornings, afternoons or evenings?"*
- *"We should get started right away so we can start working toward your goals. How's Monday at 7 AM for you?"*
- *"Let's get started immediately."*
- *"Let's book for tomorrow morning."*
- *"I can schedule you in every Tuesday at 9."*
- *"Do you want to work with me?"*
- *"Do you want me to help you get the results you want?"*
- *"Are you ready to start working toward achieving your goals?"*
- *"Based on your goals, I think we should try a 15-session package."*

You've got to ask for business. Once you're finished with the movement aspect of the session, sit down and review the entire program and the suggested plan for success. You may say something like:

"John, I'm so glad we were able to start you off with 4 key abdominal exercises. You can start on those immediately. You've also told me it's important to you to tackle fat loss. I can definitely help design a program that includes aerobic exercise, muscle conditioning and proper nutrition— all key components of an effective fat-loss program. There are lots of ways you and I can work together toward your goals. Some of my clients see me as often as 5 times a week and others as little as once every 2 weeks. It depends on how much time and, of course, money they want to commit to their goals. What do you think would work for you?"

Once you have asked the client for a commitment, stop talking and wait for a response. Sales experts suggest that people need 3 to 4 seconds before they can respond.

Remember to look for signs that the prospect is telling you she wants to invest in your services (e.g., her checkbook or day planner comes out). Timing is everything. Don't ramble on with more information if the client is ready to sign up. If you wait too long, she may change her mind. Have you ever been in a situation where you were ready to buy and the salesperson was still trying to sell you? If your client is ready to buy, let her buy.

Answering Concerns and Objections

Almost any objection to purchasing sessions can be dealt with in a soft, nonaggressive but assertive manner. Success with objections starts with showing more value than risk to personal training with you. With personal training, "No" generally means "I don't know." People come to you because they are interested.

When handling a concern or an objection, try the following system:

1. Listen to the entire concern.

2. Show understanding.

3. Ask questions.

4. Give information.

5. Convince the client you can help.

The following scenarios give some ideas for responding to common client concerns.

Concern: "I'll never stick to it."

"You're concerned about sticking to the program. I can understand that, and that's why you need a personal trainer, Sam. I will design a routine that will help you achieve the results you want. I will regularly update your program to give you variety and keep you challenged. And, of course, you'll have me to keep you motivated and on track."

Or

"Julie, at first, a lot of my other clients were concerned about sticking to the program, too, but it's now become a habit for them. In just a few months, exercise will become a part of your routine, the same as taking a shower or brushing your teeth. The results you see will really keep you motivated. And, Julie, it's my job to make sure you stick to it!"

Or

"Joe, that's the beauty of personal training. When you make an appointment with me, it's an appointment you can't miss—just like a doctor's appointment. So you're forced to stick to your goals. If you don't make it for an appointment, I'll be calling and demanding to know why! You can't lose!"

Concern: "I can't afford it."

"I can respect that you want to make sure you get the best value for your money. Let's review your goals and what personal training can offer you so you can decide for yourself." [Remind her of everything she wants to accomplish and how personal training will help her achieve those things.] *"Wouldn't you agree that your health and fitness are worth a small investment?"*

Or

"I have many clients who were in the same situation, but then they realized that the average person spends at least $50 on incidental items like fast food, entertainment and dinners. Jill, you don't need to spend any more than you're already spending. All you need to do is invest in something that's really important to you."

Or

"Bill, I really want to help you achieve your goals and I can accommodate any financial situation. Not all my clients see me every week. If you can't afford that, why don't we see each other once every 2 weeks or maybe once a month? That way, at least I can help you move toward your goals. Don't you think your goals are worth investing in one session every month?"

Provide other options, such as partner or group training. Suggest meeting twice a week for only half-hour sessions instead of hour sessions.

Concern: "I don't have the time."

"I can understand your concerns about time. That's exactly why personal training is for you. Working with a personal trainer will ensure that you don't waste any time in the gym, and you get maximum results from your workouts. It's the results that interest you, right?"

Or

"I know that your health and appearance are important to you—that's why personal training is perfect for you. All you have to do is show up for the session. I'll have everything ready to go and a program that will get results quickly. Don't you think that will save you a lot of time?"

Or

"I can certainly understand that your time is valuable and you want to make the best use of it! In fact, a lot of my clients feel exactly the same way. They all have work, family and social commitments that compete for their time, leaving very little time for workouts. But they've found that exercise is what holds everything together for them. It keeps them sane! Their exercise program gives them more energy, greater confidence and a higher level of stamina. When they exercise, they feel more productive, so they get things done more quickly, with time left to enjoy the finer things in life. Wouldn't you love to have more energy and be more productive in your life? Good! You just have to choose your priorities."

Concern: "I want to think about it."

"I'm glad you want to think this over, Alex. It shows me you take this decision seriously. Let's review some of the things we've talked about so you can make a more informed decision." [Remind him of everything he wants to accomplish and how the benefits of personal training outweigh the benefits of exercising on his own.] *"In view of all this, it sounds like you've already made the logical decision. Is there anything else stopping you from starting your exercise program?"*

Or

"You mentioned that you've been thinking about personal training and achieving these goals for some time. Do you realize that if you had started when you first began thinking about it, you would already have the results we've talked about? Imagine how good you'd feel! Let's get you started today so you can start seeing those results soon!"

Concern: "What are your prices?"

You will get this question often. Before you answer it, discuss the potential client's history and goals, and provide an action plan. Then you can comfortably offer her training options and price packages, because her decision will be based not only on prices but also on the relationship you have just developed. The conversation starts with the client saying something like this: "Hi. I would like to know how much personal training costs." You could answer:

"Well, that depends on your goals. We have a variety of personal training packages to meet anyone's situation. Let me ask you a couple of questions so I can better direct you. Are you exercising now? Really, how often? Excellent! Do you have any injuries I should know about? . . . "

Concern: "I'd like to purchase just one session."

A potential client may not understand what personal training is all about and may really believe she can get everything she needs by investing in only one session. Of course, we know this is not realistic. Be honest. Inform her that one session is not enough time to design a solid program that includes cardiovascular training; muscle conditioning for the upper body, lower body and torso; and flexibility—with time left to discuss posture, nutrition and lifestyle. Let her know that after only one session she will walk away with more questions than answers and will be frustrated with the rushed process.

Explain that in the beginning it is better to invest in the process so you can design an effective program, and then she can begin training on her own. Tell her you will need 5 hours of sessions to design a complete program, and then she can begin seeing you just once or twice every 2 months.

Concern: "I'll buy a 5-session package and then follow the program on my own."

After a couple of years of following their original personal training program, clients wonder why they're no longer getting results. Right from the beginning, you need to educate each client that after about 4 to 8 weeks, her body will adapt to the program you have designed, and the program will need to be adjusted and advanced if she wants to continue experiencing positive changes.

Inform her that she will need to see you one or 2 times every one to 2 months so you can make the appropriate changes. It's also a good idea to book her for future appointments ahead of time, reserving time in your schedule, so she doesn't allow too much time to lapse between program updates. If you leave it up to your client, it may be 3 to 6 months before she returns to update her program. If she doesn't want to book ahead, make a note in your day planner to call her in about 6 weeks to book the reassessment.

Avoid Buyer's Remorse

In the fitness industry, because people are investing in something intangible, they often suffer from buyer's remorse after the purchase. They may have just invested $1,000, and they're walking away with nothing to show for it! It's not as if they can see the positive changes yet. You have to do whatever you can to convince your client that she has made the right decision. Start by affirming that decision. For example:

"Sally, you should be so pleased with yourself. Most people just think about starting an exercise program and never actually do anything about it! You are going to be so pleased with the results!"

Sending your client away with a resource package will help quiet her concerns. Inside a folder, include educational articles, testimonials and other promotional information. This gives her something to show for her investment. She can go home and look through all the material and maintain her excitement.

Telephone the client after 24 hours to say thank you. This call will take only a few seconds, and the impact is worth it. It can be as easy as leaving a message on her answering machine that says:

"Hey, Julie, it's Sherri calling. I just wanted to tell you how much I enjoyed our personal training session yesterday. I hope you're feeling pretty good. I can't wait for our appointment on Thursday—I've got some great ideas for your program and I've come up with a couple of new stretches to really help you with your golf game. Give me a call if you have any questions about anything, and have a great day!"

This type of call is important whether you've actually sold the client on more sessions or not.

After a week, send a thank-you letter. This is a small gesture that will really set you apart from other trainers. I like to send all new clients a generic letter that discusses my appreciation to them for choosing me to help them achieve their goals, and my commitment and responsibility to them and their fitness program.

November 13th, 2000

New Client
Client's Address
Client's City, State
Client's Zip Code

Dear New Client

The NorthWest Personal Training Team would like to welcome you to the program. We are honored that you have chosen us to help facilitate your quest towards improved fitness and a higher quality of life. As part of our commitment to you, we will provide you with motivation, inspiration, education, safety and the latest exercise methods and conditioning programs.

One of our highest values is Customer Service and we will strive to consistently exceed your expectations. If you have any comments, concerns or questions about any of the additional services we offer, please feel free to contact us at 360.574.7292. We look forward to helping you achieve your goals.

Thank you.

Yours in health and fitness,

NorthWest Personal Training and Fitness Education Inc.

Alex   Sherri   Toni   Rob

Your Personal Trainers,
Alex & Sherri McMillan
Rob Cloke
Toni Egger

Advisory Board Members

DR. WAYNE LATIMER, D.C.
Chiropractic Care and Sports Medicine

SHARON FROBERG
EMT, LMP, NCTMB Massage Therapy

TINA SAKER, P.T.
Physical Therapy

MIKE & DARLENE PARNELL, B.A.
Marketing

LARRY E. KJELDEN, EA, ABA
Accounting

JEROME F. ELINE, J.D.
Legal

RUSS DYER, B.S.
Community Relations

Looking Good & Feeling Great!

New Client,
You are going to be so impressed with the results after 10 weeks. Remember your goals: 8+ glasses of H₂O every day, 20 strength training workouts and 30 cardio workouts by January 31st. See you on Monday.
Sherri

Training Center located at PRINCETON Vancouver's Athletic Club • 805 Broadway, Vancouver WA 98660 • info@NWPersonalTraining.com • www.NWPersonalTraining.com
office: 360.574.7292 • club: 360.696.0231 • f. 360.574.7283 • e. info@NWPersonalTraining.com

Most people know that letters received from businesses are computer generated and that everybody gets the same one. So I always include a handwritten personalized "P.S." at the bottom of each letter. For example:

"Sally, I can tell from your positive attitude that you are ready to make the changes necessary to improve your health and maximize fat loss. I commend you for making this commitment to yourself, and I'm so looking forward to helping you achieve all your goals! It's me and you every Tuesday and Thursday at 9:00 AM from now on. Here's to reaching for the stars!"

Send this letter whether or not the client has signed up for more sessions. If you haven't yet convinced the client to purchase, this follow-up may impress her into signing up. I am including a copy of the letter we send to all new clients.

Becoming a successful trainer involves 3 stages: getting potential clients interested, convincing them you can help when they invest in your services and, finally, keeping them. It boils down to marketing, selling and customer service.

CHAPTER FOURTEEN
Going the Distance

"It is the experience of those who have tried it, that working from a sense of duty, working for the work's sake, working as a service, instead of for a living,. . . brings blessings into the life."
Henry T. Hamblin

I've developed the ability to keep my clients for a long time. Yet I know my exercise programs are no better than any other personal trainer's exercise programs. So why do clients choose to continue training with me for extended periods of time? I must be giving them something more than just an exercise program! If you want to succeed in the personal training industry, you need to know how to get clients in the door; convince them to invest in your services; and, finally, keep them as ongoing, long-term clients.

There are many systems you can implement to ensure you are continuously exceeding your clients' expectations. When you focus on retaining your present clients, they will be so impressed with your services they will brag about you to everyone they know. Attention to small details is critical to both retaining your present clients and obtaining frequent referrals from them. The little things count: motivational phone calls, letters, birthday cards, surprise notes on workout cards, educational handouts, informational e-mails, postcards, cool new equipment and exercises. Your clients want to know you care about them. Get to know their families. Host client parties and events. Have a customer service plan and follow it—with no exceptions.

You have an incredible opportunity to make a difference in your clients' lives. Think of that before each session. Learn to make your clients' training sessions the best part of their day! Always look for, and point out, success. For example:

- "Last week you did 12 reps and today you did 14."
- "Last week you were at level 3 and today you were at level 4."

- "When you first started with me, you could lift only 5 pounds. Now you're lifting 15. That's amazing!"
- "Last week you could manage only 8 minutes and today you did 12."

You may not realize it, but you are in a position to develop your clients' feelings of self-worth and self-confidence. This is the best part of your job—when clients start to feel better about themselves and you know you've played a small part in that.

Take Care of Yourself!

In our industry we give and give. We have to be positive and upbeat at all times. And at the end of the week we can be exhausted. The burnout rate in our industry is high, so you have to figure out what it's going to take to keep you fresh and excited. For some trainers, a short holiday once every 3 to 4 months is rejuvenating. Others balance their schedules. For instance, they may work early mornings 3 times a week and evenings 2 times a week, and then take the weekends off. Other trainers refuse to work split days. Some enjoy a massage once a week to help them relax. Others meditate or pray. Some stay excited by attending workshops or conferences. Figure out what it's going to take for you—and do it.

Planning to Succeed

When you want to build a house, you don't just start building. You begin with an architectural plan so you know before you start exactly what the house will look like. Once you're clear about the finished product, you lay the foundation and work up from that base.

In the same manner, owners of successful personal training businesses develop a solid plan and lay a foundation to build on. They are crystal clear on the details of their marketing plans, sales systems and customer service programs.

I hope this workbook has helped you develop that plan and lay that foundation.

I wish you lots of success, peace and happiness. And I desire that you will all become "wealthy" personal trainers in all senses of the word: physically, spiritually and mentally. For we all know that true wealth is not monetary—it's much greater than that!

Keep on making a difference in people's lives.

CHAPTER FIFTEEN
Profiles of Success

"If you approach the ocean with a cup, you can only take away a cupful; if you
approach it with a bucket you can take away a bucketful."

Ramana Maharshi

One of the beauties of our industry is that it is so diversified. We can all do something different and all do very well. This verifies the abundance theory: There is enough room at the top for all of us.

Following are profiles of personal training businesses that contain various marketing mixes of product, price, promotion and place. When gathering this information, I noted that the most productive source of new clients was word-of-mouth referrals. This fact reaffirms everything we've learned so far. Do your best to exceed your clients' expectations, and service them so well that they brag about you to everybody they know.

Model: Personal Training Business Within a Fitness Club

Business:
The Fitness Group
Vancouver, British Columbia

Contact:
Julie McNeney

Nature of the Business:
- 8,500-square-foot fitness-only facility
- 1,800-square-foot private training studio
- Personal training for 10+ years, fitness club for 20+ years
- 12 personal trainers

Type of Client:

- Beginners, clients in injury rehab, and intermediate/advanced and sport-specific exercisers
- Focus predominantly on weight loss
- 80% women, 20% men

Advertising/Marketing:

- Yellow pages
- Direct mail
- Web site
- Medical referrals ("We operate a Physiotherapy and Massage Therapy Clinic that is closely linked to the medical community. We may get 3-4 medical referrals a month.")
- Word-of-mouth referrals ("Our greatest source of new clients")

Economics and Packaging of Services:

- Average Can.$54 per session
- Packages with varied pricing
- Partner, group (3, 4, 10), at home, sport-specific and outdoor training; training based on the methods of Joseph Pilates
- 300-400 active clients, 200 inactive clients
- Can.$450,000 personal training revenue generated per year

Model: Personal Training Business Within a Fitness Club

Business:

Active Fitness
North Ryde, New South Wales, Australia

Contact:

Justin Tamsett

Nature of the Business:

- 1,100-square-meter fitness-only center
- 8 personal trainers

Type of Client:

- Some beginners
- Lack motivation and want to be pushed
- Focus on weight loss
- Want assistance with resistance training
- 80% women, 20% men

Niche Service:
- 30-minute sessions incorporating strength and flexibility and neck/upper-back massage ("This is a unique type of training in our area.")

Advertising/Marketing:
- Internal newsletter and posters
- Word-of-mouth referrals
- Potential clients seeing sessions in action (trainers wear a uniform on the gym floor)
- Free massages for members who introduce new clients
- Monthly specials for clients (20% off in the pro shop, 2-for-1 nutrition consultations, etc.)
- Web site (gained 1 client over 12 months from this source)
- Best promotional offer: 4 sessions for Aus.$99 (savings of Aus.$35)

Customer Service:
- Quarterly newsletter to all current and ex-clients
- Water bottle and towel provided for clients at each session

Economics and Packaging of Services:
- Aus.$60 for 1-hour personal training session
- Aus.$34 the starting rate for 30-minute session
- Packages with varied pricing
- 1 complimentary session for all members
- "Tender Loving Care" program (membership package), with 8 training sessions
- 360+ thirty-minute sessions and 20 one-hour sessions each month
- 120 active clients, 105 inactive clients
- Profit margin about 20%; projected at 35% by the end of 2001
- Aus.$120,000 generated in 1999; goal of Aus.$200,000 in 2000

Model: Personal Training Business Within a Fitness Club

Business:
GoodLife Fitness Clubs
London, Ontario

Contact:
Michele Colwell

Nature of the Business:

- Chain of 50 full-service fitness clubs
- 5,000-60,000 square feet each (average = 15,000-20,000 square feet)
- In operation for 21 years
- Separate line of equipment exclusively for trainers at a few clubs
- 250 personal trainers altogether

Type of Client:

- Beginners, plateau exercisers, and clients with back or knee injuries
- Focus on weight loss
- 70-75% women, 25-30% men (some clubs 60% women, 40% men)

Niche Services:

- 6-week fat-loss program, with full meal plan, 18 half-hour workouts (3 times a week) with a personal trainer, guaranteed results or money refunded
- 6-week "Reshape" program, with complete fitness appraisal, 1-hour workout 2 times a week with a personal trainer, and supplements (vitamins, minerals and Super Reshape formula)
- 6-week golf conditioning program
- 6-week "Learn to Run" program

Advertising/Marketing:

- Direct mail
- Before-and-after success stories, with banners/posters throughout club
- Signs in washroom
- Announcements in fitness classes about free sessions
- Ballot boxes in local businesses to win free personal training session
- Newspapers and magazines
- Radio talk shows
- Free training of TV personnel
- Yellow pages
- New club members contacted by personal training coordinator
- "Buddy Buck System": $50 voucher to a member who refers someone who then purchases
- Promotions: buy 5 personal training sessions get 1 free; buy 10, get 2; buy 20, get 3
- Approximately Can.$4-6 discount for every increment in number of sessions per package
- Word-of-mouth referrals (largest source of new clients)

Customer Service:

- Motivational calls from personal trainers to check on progress/satisfaction and attempt to book an appointment to address clients' specific challenges
- Birthday cards, member appreciation parties, invitations to special events, etc.

Economics and Packaging of Services:
- Can.$35-$75 for 1-hour session
- Can.$29-$59 for ½-hour session

Model: Personal Training Business Within a Fitness Club

Business:
Sweat Co Studio Ltd.
Vancouver, British Columbia

Contact:
Maureen Wilson

Nature of the Business:
- 7,800-square-foot fitness-only studio
- In business for 16 years
- 6 personal trainers

Type of Client:
- Sport-specific and plateau exercisers and lots of beginners
- 70% women, 30% men

Advertising/Marketing:
- Yellow pages
- Articles ("The media come to us.")
- Downtown location (attracts out-of-town clients)
- Reputation as a dance-based studio (attracts theater and film crews)
- Word-of-mouth referrals (source of most new clients)
- Celebrity training ("Training celebrities has brought us some business, but we try to be discreet, and they appreciate this.")

Customer Service:
- Money provided for parking meters, dinner reservations made, and many other courtesy services provided ("Our front desk managers are almost like a concierge. Most clients come to us because they enjoy a more personal touch and don't mind spending a little more.")
- Free water and towel for each session

Economics and Packaging of Services:
- Average Can.$60 per session
- Packages with varied pricing
- 3,900 clients in 1999
- 380-460 sessions per month
- Can.$260,000-$275,000 generated in 1999

Model: Personal Training Business Within a Fitness Club

Business:

City Personal Training Pty Ltd.
Melbourne, Victoria, Australia

Contact:

Nikki Ellis

Nature of the Business:

- 30- to 40-square-meter personal training studio within a mid-sized club
- 5 years of personal training (started building the business after 4 years)
- 8 personal trainers

Type of Client:

- 90% beginners or clients with a bit of experience; 5% sport-specific and 5% postrehab clients
- 76% women, 24% men

Advertising/Marketing:

- Yellow pages
- Internal club newsletter, posters, brochures
- Web site
- Potential clients seeing sessions in action (get 41% of clients this way— "Our best advertising is our bright uniform with our company name on it! Since we introduced these uniforms, there has been a substantial increase in personal training sales.")
- Word-of-mouth referrals (main source of new clients)
- Annual mailing to current clients of 2 laminated passes for ½ -hour personal training sessions for friends and loved ones ("Our clients love this and place value on having a laminated card they can carefully give out!")
- 1-2 referrals a month from sports and spinal medicine clinic located directly below health club
- Seminars, e.g., "Women and Weights," "Eating to Stay Lean," etc. ("Seminars are the best way for us to instantly gain 10 new clients. We advertise in the local paper, and at the end of the seminar circulate a sign-up sheet for a complimentary session. The next day we do a follow-up call and the clients start coming in.")
- Leads from in-house sales staff for complimentary personal training sessions

Customer Service:

- Christmas and birthday cards
- Newsletter

Economics and Packaging of Services:
- 1-hour session, Aus.$42 for facility members, $45 for nonmembers
- 5 sessions, Aus.$210 for members and nonmembers
- 8 half-hour sessions, Aus.$239 for members, $279 for nonmembers
- 94 active clients, 26 inactive clients
- 359 one-hour sessions performed each month
- Approx. Aus.$150,000 yearly gross revenue predicted

Model: Personal Training Studio
Business:
Sports Reaction Center
Bellevue, Washington

Contact:
Neil Chasan

Nature of the Business:
- 2,000-square-foot physical therapy clinic and training center
- In business for 19 years

Type of Client:
- Sport-specific exercisers, beginners and postrehab clients
- 60% women, 40% men

Niche Services:
- Golf-specific training
- Functional rehab

Advertising/Marketing:
- Primarily referrals from physicians and golf professionals (practice is almost 100% physician-referral-based)
- Word-of-mouth referrals
- Sponsorships ("We sponsored a golf tournament this year and we sponsor a couple of Olympic-class runners.")
- Web site that is easy to maintain and update (draws a lot of attention from active people)

Economics and Packaging of Services:
- U.S.$100 for 1-hour session
- About 5 new clients each week
- About 100 active clients
- Over 200 personal training sessions performed every month

Model: Training in Clients' Homes or Other Locations

Business:

On The Edge Fitness Consulting
Vancouver, British Columbia

Contact:

Donna Hutchinson

Nature of the Business:

- Sessions outdoors, in clients' homes and community centers
- Sole proprietorship since June 1999
- Self and 1 trainer
- Personal trainer for 7 years

Type of Client:

- New exercisers, most with a medical condition (arthritis, cerebral palsy, fibromyalgia, osteoporosis, cancer, back injuries)
- Lack motivation
- Definitely desire weight loss
- 90% women, 10% men

Advertising/Marketing:

- Local paper—*The Courier* ("Haven't seen great results from this venue yet.")
- Yellow pages
- Writing monthly fitness tip column for a local magazine—*Shared Vision*
- Web site
- Virtual personal trainer for the Sea2summit adventure races Web site
- Guest speaker on a local TV station ("This is very helpful.")
- Word-of-mouth referrals (These generate the most business. A client who refers a friend or family member automatically receives a letter saying thank you for the referral, even if the friend doesn't sign up. If the friend does sign up, the client has the choice of a free personal training session or a spa gift.)
- Community involvement and networking (have worked the best for developing the business)

Customer Service:

- Referral incentives
- Indoor climbing events
- Ongoing client handouts
- Quarterly client newsletter
- Renewal thank-you letters
- Birthday cards, flowers, candy

Economics and Packaging of Services:

- Average Can.$55 for 1-hour session
- Partner training, group training, at-home training, hiking day, "Climb the Grouse Grind," indoor rock climbing, inline skating
- Group training/partner training discounts for long-term clients
- 30 active clients, 30 inactive clients
- 125 sessions a month
- Over Can.$30,000 generated in first 6 months of business

Model: Training in Clients' Homes or Other Locations

Business:

Fitness by Colin Westerman
Vancouver, British Columbia

Contact:

Colin Westerman

Nature of the Business:

- Independent contractor in studios, clubs, people's homes and outdoors
- Personal trainer for 4 years

Type of Client:

- Beginners, plateau exercisers, baby boomers exercising for health as opposed to aesthetics, and sport-specific clients
- 50% women, 50% men

Niche Services:

- Training for golf
- Nutrition consulting

Advertising/Marketing:

- Business cards
- Word-of-mouth referrals (largest source of new clients—"I offer a free session to [each client] who refers a client who signs up. I also send a thank-you card and a small gift.")
- Newspaper and magazine articles
- Fitness expert on a morning TV show

Customer Service:

- Birthday cards and gifts
- Frequent exerciser discounts
- Weekly e-mail tips and weekly goals sent to active clients every Monday morning
- Fresh towel every workout

Economics and Packaging of Services:

- Can.$45-$55 for 1-hour session
- Can.$60 for nutrition consultation
- 25 active clients, 15 inactive clients
- 70 personal training sessions monthly
- Can.$35,000/year generated as personal training revenue

Model: Training in Clients' Homes or Other Locations

Business:

FIT-JETS
Toyooka-shi, Hyogo-ken, Japan

Contact:

Ingrid Knight-Cohee

Nature of the Business:

- Virtual training
- Personal trainer for 6 years

Type of Client:

- Plateau exercisers and, occasionally, sport-specific clients
- Interested in losing body fat, learning about healthy eating with new and foreign food choices
- 80% women, 20% men

Niche Service:

- Catering to the unique circumstances of foreigners, usually from western, English-speaking countries, who live and work in Japan (Owner lived in Japan for 3 years and is expanding virtual training services to a broader clientele.— "Japan-based foreigners live either in a remote area with no facilities, or an urban area where the cost of club membership makes a facility inaccessible. I often create home workouts and provide dietary recommendations through regular e-mail correspondence and a Web site with articles and fitness links.")

Advertising/Marketing:

- 2 Web sites (1 personal, the other in connection with thepersonaltrainer.net)
- Fitness articles in local monthly and bimonthly newsletters
- E-mailing and faxing to a list of foreigners

Economics and Packaging of Services:

- Can.$30 equivalent for a single virtual training program
- Can.$20/month equivalent for motivational contact and program upgrades
- 10 active virtual training clients

Index

About the Author

Sherri McMillan, MSc, has been in the fitness industry for over 17 years and has been nominated for and awarded various fitness industry awards, including 1998 IDEA International Personal Trainer of the Year, 1998 CanFitPro Canadian Fitness Presenter of the Year, 2005 ACE Fitness Educator of the Year Runner-Up and 2005 IDEA Fitness Director of the Year Finalist. She has authored four books: *Go For Fit: The Winning Way to Fitness; Successful Trainer's Guide to Marketing; Hiring & Training Master Trainers;* and *Fit over Forty: The Winning Way to Lifetime Fitness.* She has presented hundreds of workshops to thousands of fitness leaders throughout Canada, Australia, New Zealand, Germany, England, Spain, South America, Asia and the U.S.A., including the prestigious IDEA, CanFitPro and IHRSA conferences. She is a Nike, Spri, Fitter International, Nautilus and PowerBar sponsored fitness athlete and is a fitness columnist for various newspapers, magazines and journals throughout the world. With her husband Alex, she is the co-owner of NorthWest Personal Training and Fitness Education, a personal training studio and education center in Vancouver, Washington and Portland, Oregon.